Successful Youth Mentoring

Loveland, Colorado

Successful Youth Mentoring

Copyright © 1998 Emerging Young Leaders

Credits

Contributing Authors: Dr. Keith Drury, Bill Eakin, Tim Elmore, Andy Fletcher, Steve Gardner, Dr. Tim Mills, Dr. Art O'Dell, Dave Scherer, Dan Seaborn, Dr. Richard Wynn, Gail Zainea
Executive Editor: Dr. Richard R. Wynn
General Editor: Dr. Art O'Dell
Content Editor: Steve Gardner
Final Editor: Dean Merrill
Art Director: Kari K. Monson
Cover Art Director: Jeff A. Storm
Computer Graphic Artist: Randy Kady
Cover Designer: D² Designworks
Illustrator: Amy Bryant
Production Manager: Gingar Kunkel

Unless otherwise noted, Scripture taken from the HOLY BIBLE, NEW INTERNATIONAL VERSION®. Copyright © 1973, 1978, 1984 by International Bible Society. Used by permission of Zondervan Publishing House. All rights reserved.

Scripture quotations marked "NLT" are from the New Living Translation © 1996 Tyndale Charitable Trust.

Library of Congress Cataloging-in-Publication Data
Successful youth mentoring / [by Keith Drury ... et al.].
    p.   cm.
  ISBN 0-7644-2104-2
  1. Youth--Counseling of--Handbooks, manuals, etc. 2. Mentoring--Handbooks, manuals, etc. I. Drury, Keith W.
  HV1421.S83 1998
  259'.23--dc21
                                        98-16966
                                        CIP

10 9 8 7 6 5 4 3 2 1   07 06 05 04 03 02 01 00 99 98

Printed in the United States of America.

Contents

Introduction: Making the Most of This Material

Congratulations on your decision to invest in the lives of others through the mutually enriching experience of mentoring. We want to make this as rewarding as possible for you. Please take a few minutes to read this introduction. We've made it brief, but it should relieve initial apprehensions as well as later frustration and disappointment. Having a clear idea of both the goal and process will enable you to achieve maximum results with a minimum of frustration.

Top Ten Reasons to Mentor

1. Instill values in your mentees.
2. Develop their leadership skills.
3. Open their minds to greater possibilities.
4. Increase their self-image through your willingness to invest time.
5. Counsel them on life's critical issues.
6. Encourage service and a giving mentality (you model this by mentoring).
7. Decrease self-centeredness (for all involved).
8. Strengthen your relationship.
9. Obey scriptural commands (Ephesians 6:3).
10. Increase the value of your life by leaving a legacy.

We have designed this manual to develop leadership qualities in teenage young people. The focus, however, is not just on those who have already demonstrated leadership tendencies. We know that only a small percentage of young people will rise to significant corporate or political leadership, but we also know that character-based leadership qualities are needed by all.

Mere graduation from high school doesn't adequately prepare anyone for the level of independence and the array of choices that accompany college, military service, or the adult work force. And certainly the complexities and the pace of the world today require significant leadership to successfully rear a family.

> Throughout this book, we have used the term "mentee." This term refers to the young person who is being mentored by an adult.

Top Ten Suggestions for Mentoring

1. Pray frequently for your mentees. Be specific.
2. Try to make the sessions as interesting as possible for your mentees, but don't be surprised or discouraged if they don't communicate great excitement.
3. Read at least a week ahead. That will give you time to digest the material and bring into focus current situations that could be useful.
4. Prepare in advance. Some optional experiences will require planning.
5. Pray about (and during) each mentoring session.

6. Let your mentees discover as much as possible through questions and discussion as opposed to merely "telling" them everything.

7. If your schedule requires missing a week, pick up where you left off. Try to not miss any sessions.

8. A casual atmosphere is a good idea—breakfast at a pancake house or lunch at a fast-food restaurant might be a welcome change of pace for a session that doesn't require special supplies.

9. The time of the meeting could vary each week, but set it in advance and try to start and end on time. Punctuality is a strong leadership value.

10. Maintain confidentiality with things your mentees say. You might be surprised at their sensitivity to hearing their remarks surface from some other source. If you have multiple mentees, encourage them to keep confidences as well.

Although your mentees may never be aware of the superstructure on which this entire manual hangs, we thought you might like to know that it's based on what we call the six characteristics of servant leadership: character, courage, compassion, competency, conviction, and commitment. Each of the four series in this year of curriculum lasts six weeks and includes a session on each of the six characteristics. We recommend a break of one to three weeks between each series.

Whether you follow our suggested timetable or modify it to accommodate your specific needs, we're confident that you'll experience a healthy balance of leadership teaching based on important character qualities.

Top Ten Mistakes Mentors Make

1. Failure to start
2. Thinking they must master these principles before they can share them
3. Unwillingness to make mentoring a high priority so that time is regularly scheduled
4. Thinking that the sessions must occur in a formal or academic setting
5. Failure to pray regularly for their mentees
6. Using parental authority in a heavy-handed way when mentoring their own children
7. Unwillingness to be transparent and vulnerable
8. Making the session longer than the interest span of their mentees
9. Turning the session into a lecture or a sermon rather than a quality exchange
10. Expecting to see immediate and/or unrealistic changes in their mentees

---

This last section is especially important. Please review it carefully.

Top Ten Clarifications and Instructions

1. The learning options in this book include a wide variety of activities, from discussion starters to stories to field trips. If it seems appropriate to your mentoring relationship, try to use a wide variety of options to keep the experiences fresh and exciting.

2. It is normal to begin this process with some degree of fear and feeling of inadequacy. Some of the leadership principles may be new to you. So much the better—you and your mentees can learn together.

3. This manual is for mentors. It is not a workbook for mentees. We have deliberately avoided a workbook approach that mentees might resent as being too much like a classroom experience. The best mentoring relies heavily on the natural relationship and exchange between mentor and mentee. The role of this guide is to give some content and handles to enhance that exchange.

4. We have developed a one-on-three mentoring model that offers several advantages over the traditional one-on-one. You will notice the frequent use of the plural "mentees" throughout this manual. You might consider mentoring more than one young person at a time—perhaps the addition of someone from a single-parent home. Be assured that the sessions are equally valid for either single or multiple mentees.

5. If you choose to mentor more than one young person at a time, try to form a group of young people similar in age and interests if possible.

6. We have attempted to make this manual gender-neutral so that it can be used comfortably by either sex.

7. You will notice multiple options in many sections of most sessions. These attempt to account for diversity in age, interest, personality, and gender of mentees. Choose from among them to tailor the session for your mentees. Feel free to modify or even invent your own options.

8. The "Ancient Wisdom" section of each session includes a verse to remember. We strongly recommend this as a verse to memorize. However, we also strongly recommend that it not be handled in such a way that mentees become hesitant to come to the next session if they haven't memorized their verse from the last one. It might be helpful if the mentor commits to memorizing the verse as well.

9. The illustrations that appear throughout the manual are geared for a youthful audience. You may ignore them entirely, or you may use them as a guide to doodle or sketch a visual aid during your session.

10. Always keep in mind that sharing from your personal experience is valuable. Being willing to admit past mistakes and what you learned from them is usually more effective than relating success stories. It encourages your mentees to know that they are not alone in making mistakes and that mistakes are not the end of the world. In fact, they can be great learning experiences.

The entire Emerging Young Leaders family joins me in wishing you God's best as you begin this awesome task of mentoring young people. We have prayed and will continue to pray for God's blessing in your lives.

Dr. Richard R. Wynn, President
Emerging Young Leaders, Inc.

What Mentoring Is All About

Today's young people have all the questions, tensions, and awkwardness kids have always had growing through adolescence and trying to establish their own identities. But now they also face much more. The current American youth culture is filled with expensive toys, unparalleled freedom, access to drugs of all kinds, sophisticated and attractive media filled with unhealthy messages, a prevailing societal attitude that teen sex is inevitable, frequent exposure to every temptation on earth, and less input from parents than ever before imaginable.

Your choice to intentionally mentor one or more young people will most likely begin a chain reaction of events that will long outlive you. Not until eternity will you discover all the ripple effects of your actions and the answers to the "what if we hadn't?" questions.

Are You Qualified?

At this point you may be feeling something between excitement and apprehension. If you're like most people, you think you have something to offer, but you fear you may not be able to deliver the goods. Let us tell you a little bit about the necessary qualifications of a mentor.

Perhaps the best way to begin is with a quick three-part exercise.

Thinking back on your own life, who, other than your parents, has influenced you the most? Stop for a minute and review your past until you have a face locked in your mind.

Now make a quick list of the qualities that enabled that person to make an impact on you. What did that person have or do that drew you to him or her and resulted in positive change on your part? Within a minute or two, you should have a list of several things.

Look at your list. How many of those are more attitude than aptitude? Probably at least 80 percent of the items on your list are things like integrity, sincerity, commitment, consistency, wisdom (at least a little beyond what you had at the time), love, generosity, and perseverance.

Do you see the point? The issue is not so much "Can you mentor successfully?" as it is "Will you?" The people who have had great impact on you have not necessarily been in the genius category. Nor did most of them have earned doctorates in esoteric subjects. They cared, they were available, they had learned to deal with issues that matter in life, and they were willing to share their experiences. Can you do that? Of course you can. Will you do that? That's the $64,000 question.

The Mentoring Commitment

Here are the three basic commitments of being a mentor.

Commitment to the person—This may seem fairly obvious, but we all tend to get caught up in the "bigger is better" syndrome. We want to reach the masses. Have you noticed that the Bible is filled with paradoxes? Dawson Trotman, founder of the Navigators, put his finger on this one, which is never actually stated in Scripture, but which is demonstrated through the ministry strategy of Jesus: More time with fewer people equals greater impact for God's kingdom.

You can impress a lot of people in one shot, but when it comes to sharing life experience, application, and accountability—that's a deeper approach. Are you satisfied with relationships that are a mile wide and an inch deep? Probably not. You need to be committed to a person. And the genius of this paradox is that when you invest your life in the lives of two or three others, that investment multiplies and the width takes care of itself.

Commitment to the process—As you have worked to master a new skill or principle, have you ever felt like a pinball being knocked around until you finally got it? It may have taken you several steps to get from point A to point D, right? And it may have taken you several days, weeks, months, or even years. Why should we expect our mentees to get there overnight? Mentors must develop a "process mentality."

Recognize that to get from point A to point D requires at least taking steps B and C, even in the most direct path. And there most likely will be an excursion or two along the way—learning is often like that. But the process will be quicker and less painful because of your input.

Commitment to the purpose—Can you remember times when you have come alongside other people and naturally begun to play a mentoring role? You probably saw potential in them, some hidden gold, that they hadn't fully realized. You encouraged them to do something they thought they couldn't do.

Many people haven't yet brought their abilities into focus. Until they internalize the fact that God has uniquely gifted them, they need to be lovingly pushed. That's much of what mentoring is about.

What Really Counts

Have you seen the movie *Mr. Holland's Opus?* It's the story of a reluctant mentor. Mr. Holland had no intention of being a mentor—he wanted to be a musician. In fact, he wanted to go to New York and compose and perform and be famous.

In the meantime, though, he decided to teach high school for three years to earn enough money to pursue his dream. He quickly discovered that teaching wasn't quite what he had envisioned it would be. He came home and told his wife, "I hate teaching, Iris, I hate it. Nobody can teach these children, nobody!" But the time to make the break never seemed to arrive. The rising cost of living, the birth of his child, the unexpected time demands of teaching—they all complicated his plan.

As time has a way of doing, the three years turned into thirty. At some point in the frustrating process, he found that he was falling in love with the students. He saw needs, and he tried to help meet them. There was the red-haired girl who desperately wanted to play the clarinet, but could produce only ugly squeaks. Mr. Holland began teaching her after school, and he discovered that the real issue was not the instrument—it was self-esteem.

He met with other kids who were on the verge of one failure or another. He hated it, and yet along the way he was driven by a need to pass on everything he could to these students. He ended up spending long hours—in fact, his very life—in that high school.

One day the principal called Mr. Holland into the office to give him some bad news. He showed him the plan he had come up with to meet the required 10 percent budget cut. The entire art, drama, and music programs would be disappearing with the stroke of a pen. Mr. Holland's teaching career was over.

He didn't know whether to throw something or to cry. He couldn't believe it had all come down to that moment. Going back to his empty music room, he sat alone in the dark until his buddy came in—the gym teacher and coach whose programs had not been cut. The coach sat down, and after a brief conversation, he said, "They have no idea how much they're going to miss you around here."

Mr. Holland disagreed. "I got dragged into this gig kicking and screaming, and now it's the only thing I want to do...you work your whole life, you work for thirty years because you think that what you do makes a difference—you think it matters to people. Then you wake up one morning and find out...you're expendable." He felt as if he had given it all for nothing. Nothing. Nobody cared. Nobody would even remember. It was all over.

Sometime later he walked down the long, empty school hall for the last time with his wife and his son. On the way out, as he walked through the lobby, he heard noise coming from the auditorium. He was curious about what could be going on since school was over for the summer, so he decided to check it out.

He opened the door to the auditorium and saw that it was full of people: alumni from all his former classes—dating back to 1963—hundreds of them, waiting for his entrance. They had come to say thanks. And that little red-haired clarinet player he had mentored was there—she was now the state governor.

The governor walked to the podium and said, "Rumor had it [Mr. Holland] was always working on this symphony of his. And this was going to make him famous, rich, probably both. But Mr. Holland isn't rich, and he isn't famous—at least not outside of our little town. So it might be easy for him to think himself a failure. And he would be wrong, because I think he's achieved a success far beyond riches and fame. Look around you. There is not a life in this room that you have not touched. And each one of us is a better person because of you. We are your symphony, Mr. Holland. We are the melodies and the notes of your opus. And we are the music of your life."

As Christians, the investments we make in the lives of others are the most significant accomplishments we'll leave behind on this earth. As we go about our daily business, it's easy to forget what really counts in the long run. But legacies are left in the hearts of people.

Gifts Mentors Give

Tim Elmore, in his book *The Greatest Mentors in the Bible*, describes seven gifts a mentor gives. These gifts are all things you could give to another person right now. Keep these in mind as you begin a mentoring relationship.

Accountability—Hold your mentees to their commitments. This may involve asking tough questions that relate to commitments they've made. You don't need new skills to do that.

Affirmation—Speak words of encouragement, acceptance, and support—affirming their strengths and their positive choices. Great mentors affirm their mentees regularly.

Assessment—Objectively evaluate their present state and give them an assessment of what you see. It enables them to gain perspective from an outside viewpoint. Think back to your adolescent years. Wouldn't you have loved it if someone had provided even just these first three gifts for you? Why are we reluctant to do this for young people?

I remember the first time I had a staff evaluation where my supervisor (and mentor) sized me up. He sat down and said, "You're really good at …and you do a great job at… "He went on with seven or eight categories like that. I was feeling really good about myself. Then he said, "Now there are just a few things we need to talk about and that you need to change." I said, "Excuse me?"

No one had ever done this for me before. He listed three things—I still remember them. That turned out to be one of the most memorable and life-changing meetings of my life because just knowing my weaknesses got me moving toward improvement. When mentors present this gift in a loving and thoughtful way, they truly can start a life-changing process in the life of a young person.

Advice—Speak words of wise counsel, and help them think through options for their decisions. You may not think of yourself as a Solomon, but you have more experience and Bible knowledge than your mentees. Be careful, though, not to go overboard on presenting advice. Sometimes all a person needs is the gift of a listening ear or a word of acceptance.

Admonition—Speak words of caution and warning. Enable your mentees to avoid pitfalls they might not see as clearly as you can. At times, they may need correction to keep them on the right, healthy path.

Assets—Give or loan tangible help in the form of books, tapes, ministry tools and other resources, personal contacts, gifts, and bright ideas. Great mentors provide assets.

Application—Help them find a laboratory where they can practice what they're learning. Good mentors suggest places where truth can be applied. And that's where the truth you help your mentees discover will become a life-changing lesson.

The Mentor's Role

Let's take a different approach for a moment and consider five powerful word pictures that help us visualize the role of a mentor. These are all tools that great mentors provide for their mentees.

Handles—Mentors help mentees internalize truth by presenting it in a way so that they can grab on to it. *Successful Youth Mentoring* does much of this for you, but you may be inspired to create some handles of your own. That's what we did with a young pastor who had never learned to share his faith.

We realized in the course of discussion that this pastor had never really developed a love and concern for people who didn't have a relationship with Jesus. So we got together with him on a Saturday morning and spent two hours at a nearby mall—not shopping. We walked from one end to the other, looking right into the eyes of everyone we passed. We tried to discern what we saw in their faces. After passing them we stopped and discussed what we had seen, making guesses about their lives and what was going on in their hearts…and we prayed for them.

Within fifteen or twenty minutes, we were crying. We were seeing older folks who were lonely, teenagers just hanging out because they didn't have anything else to do—no purpose or meaning. We were profoundly impacted by those two hours of just looking with interest and empathy into the faces of people we didn't know. We started seeing people through God's eyes.

That experience was a handle for that pastor. We'll never forget that simple morning. Anyone could have done that with this young pastor, but nobody ever had. And the experience changed his life.

Road maps—Maps show us the roads we might choose to get to a specific destination. Many times, there are multiple roads that could get us where we want to go. A road map helps us see the roads in relationship to one another so we can make informed choices, taking the best route.

"Generation X" young people really need this kind of help. Provide road maps this way: "Here are three roads you might want to take. The choice is yours. Let's talk about the consequences of taking each road. And by the way, here are three roads you might want to avoid."

Laboratories—We all need safe places to experiment with ideas and concepts we're learning. For example, suppose we extended the experience we provided for John in the mall. Suppose we spent the following Saturday morning working together on a plan for sharing our faith. We could role play to present our faith stories to each other. Sometimes a lab is just a sounding board—a safe place to think out loud and express concerns and doubts without fear of failing or being judged.

Roots—The deeper the roots grow, the taller the tree grows. Roots provide stability and security in the face of damaging winds. As the harsh winds of life blow our way, it's crucial to surround ourselves with people who will keep us grounded in the truth. Mentors can provide these roots as they speak honestly, openly, consistently, and lovingly.

Roots also provide nourishment and connection with the past. As a mentor, the better you know your mentees, the more you can help them understand their needs and their identities.

Wings—Wings are a great complement to roots because wings provide the ability to see beyond the horizon, beyond where a mentee has already been in life. The best mentors take their mentees even beyond where the mentors themselves have gone. They delight in being passed by their mentees. They realize that success without successors is failure.

Finishing the Race Together

As a mentor, you're in for an incredible journey. It may not be easy or smooth. Your mentees may fail or disappoint you from time to time, but don't forget—growth is a process.

In a way, the following true story represents the worst that can happen in a mentoring relationship—a mentee's heartbreaking failure...of sorts. Read it and decide whether the result was worth the cost.

In the 1992 Olympics in Barcelona, Derrick Redman, a runner from England, had qualified for the 440-meter race. Just qualifying was an amazing feat, since he had undergone twenty-two surgeries on his Achilles tendon. No one gave him a chance of winning. But he lined up, waved to the crowds, and drank in the excitement of this huge moment. The gun fired, and he shot out of the blocks.

Derrick was running in the middle of the pack, about halfway through the race, when he suddenly stopped short. As the TV cameras stayed focused on the front-runners, everyone assumed that Derrick Redman would not finish the race.

As soon as the winner had crossed the finish line, the cameras went back to Derrick. About thirty seconds had elapsed, and he was still far from the finish line. As the cameras rolled and a worldwide audience watched with a strange mix of horror and appreciation, Derrick began to limp toward the finish line. He had made a commitment to finish.

It was obvious that Derrick was in severe pain, and the crowds in the stands didn't know what to do. But one person chose to get involved. It was Derrick's mentor and father, Jim Redman. After all, it was Jim who had been involved all along. He had used much of his own money to finance Derrick's training. He had gotten up early on countless mornings and rode his bike while Derrick ran—timing him, encouraging him, and sometimes badgering him. And now, sitting in the next-to-last row at the top of the grandstand, his worst fears were coming true. This mentor couldn't help himself—he had to get involved.

Jim left his seat and began excusing himself as he pushed his way toward the track. "Pardon me." "Excuse me, please." "Coming through!" He ran down the steps and parted the crowds. Finally he reached the gate and pushed his way through the security guards whose job it was to keep guys like him off the track. He managed to get by them (mentors can do anything, you know) and run to his son.

Derrick tumbled into his father's arms, sobbing as they stood together on the track. Then Jim Redman did what every great mentor does. He took the arm of his mentee and put it around his own shoulder, and the two of them finished the race together.

Derrick didn't win that race, but he finished it, and he finished it well.

That's what mentoring is all about.

Getting Started

Preparing for the First Meeting

Before you begin meeting with your mentees, you'll want to work with them to make some initial plans for the relationship. Use the following guidelines in planning for the mentoring sessions.

Ask your mentees to show initiative by calling you.

This won't always work if you've agreed to work with multiple mentees. In those cases, the mentees' initial motivation may not be high enough to provide this kind of initiative. Also, depending on mentees' personalities, they may be uncomfortable calling you (if they're shy or intimidated, they're afraid of bothering you at a bad time, or they lose your number, for example). You may end up having to call your mentees, but it's a good idea to encourage them to take the initiative.

Schedule meetings in a comfortable and safe place.

Mentoring sessions can occur almost anywhere—indoors, outdoors, at home, in a church, at a restaurant, in a park, at the library…When choosing a location, consider the personality of your mentees, the weather in your area, and convenience—and don't forget about comfort. Make sure the place you choose to meet is a place your mentees will want to be.

Be aware that the content of a particular session may dictate a location with a VCR or a computer, or it may involve visiting a museum, a factory, a sporting event, a mall, or another location that will illustrate an important point. Some sessions might be of a sensitive nature and would be best conducted in a more private setting.

Meet in a predictable place at a consistent time when possible.

Freedom and creativity are two of the magic words in a good mentoring relationship, but they do require some precautions. Don't underestimate the value of meeting regularly at the same time and place. The more mentees you have and the younger they are, the more important this will be. Your mentees will face enough natural obstacles to perfect attendance; don't add more by confusing them with odd times and places.

For instance, when you choose to take a field trip as part of a session, try to meet at the normal time and place and go together from there. When that isn't possible, be sure to overcommunicate. Telephone reminders the day before are not overkill.

Determine in advance how long and how frequent your meetings will be.

We have designed each of the sessions in this book to last an hour or less, and to occur weekly in six-week units with a short break between units. Consider the needs of your mentees, your personal schedule and their schedules, and the specific goals of your mentoring relationship. Adjust the design of the meetings as necessary. Once you've determined the schedule, respect your mentees and their families by sticking with it.

The First Meeting

For your first meeting, you may be tempted to jump immediately with your mentees into the first mentoring session included in this book. We strongly recommend that your first meeting be more organizational in nature and "big picture" oriented. But it doesn't have to be dull! The following meeting plan will help you create a firm foundation and get everyone going in the same direction.

Setting Your Sights

One of the priorities in the first meeting is to establish expectations for both you and your mentees. To establish realistic and healthy expectations for the mentoring relationship, follow this suggested outline for your first meeting:

● Spend some time getting to know your mentees. Ask them about their hobbies, favorites, and interests. Find out where they go to school, what their families are like, and anything else you can. This will build the foundation of your friendship.

● Ask for mentees' top three goals in being mentored.

● Clarify your precise goals at the beginning of the relationship. Try to include as many of the mentees' goals as possible. Help them see how the mentoring process can meet their expressed needs.

● Explain your limitations of time and ability. Be realistic, but don't sell yourself short.

● Ask about their past experiences with authority. This question will help you with your expectations. It will shed some light on their view of authority, their teachability, and their willingness to take responsibility for actions rather than blaming someone else.

● Set guidelines for confidentiality. Explain to your mentees that you respect their right to privacy, and that you won't be repeating information of a sensitive nature that surfaces in your meetings. Ask them to treat you and each other with the same respect. Each one should verbally commit to this agreement.

● Pray together about your mutual goals. This is a ministry activity that bears great fruit. One of the side benefits is that your mentees will feel loved and cared for in a way that many of them desperately need. Be sure this activity doesn't stop with the first meeting, but is an ongoing element in your mentoring relationship.

Setting the Standard

Spend a few minutes explaining the qualities of mentors and mentees that we describe in our mentor-training workshops. Tell your mentees that with God's help, you and they can demonstrate these qualities consistently in your mentoring relationship. These qualities fit nicely into two easy-to-remember acrostics: GOALS and FAITH.

Qualities of Mentors

God-centered

Mentors must demonstrate Christlike character and conduct that is worth imitating. They should strive to remind others of Jesus.

Objective

Mentors must be able to see strengths and weaknesses clearly and must be willing to communicate them honestly.

Authentic

Mentors must be real. Others must be able to see their humanity. They should be genuine, transparent, and open with others.

Loyal

Mentors must be loyal to others. When friendships (or mentoring relationships) are formed, mentors should be committed to them.

Servant

Mentors must be committed to giving their lives away and making investments in the lives of their mentees.

Qualities of Mentees

Faithful

Mentees must be faithful to the commitments they've made, as well as to the basics of the Christian faith.

Available

Mentees must have the time to make the relationship a priority, and they must make themselves available to growth opportunities.

Initiative

Mentees must show initiative in their desire to grow. They should be willing to take the first step without someone "holding their hand."

Teachable

Mentees must be willing to learn new truths and must be open to change. They should exhibit soft hearts instead of stubborn ones.

Hungry

Mentees must have a passion to grow and to become all that God created them to be. They should be committed to developing their leadership skills.

Committing to the Mentoring Relationship

Sometime during (or at the conclusion of) your first mentoring session, we recommend that you and your mentees spend a few minutes formalizing your commitment to the mentoring process. To help clarify this process, we've developed a "Mentoring Covenant" form (p. 18), which gives definition to the mentoring commitment. We suggest that you photocopy this form so that each of your mentees can sign a copy (along with you) and keep it.

Mentoring Covenant

Mentors commit to a modeling and teaching relationship in which they challenge and encourage mentees to develop the characteristics of servant leaders.

Mentees commit to a relationship of learning and accountability in which they are challenged and encouraged to develop the characteristics of servant leaders.

Mentor _____ Date _____

Mentee _____ Date _____

General Meeting Guidelines

The guidelines in this section apply to every mentoring meeting. Emphasize them in your first meeting, and be sure to continue to use these skills from that point on.

Setting the Tone

Once you sit down to meet with your mentees, take the initiative to set the proper tone and atmosphere. Ask about their week, and take a few moments to talk about what's been going on in their personal lives.

Be careful not to just "jump into the business." If you're prone to skip to the "business," remember that the lives of your mentees *are* the business. The following acrostic (SALT) will help you remember how to develop the right atmosphere so dialogue can flow effectively.

Say something affirming.

Ask probing questions.

Listen well.

Turn the conversation to the topic of the day.

A Word on Confidentiality

As a mentor, you must hold yourself to the highest standard of confidentiality. You may know other mentors in your church, and you may have occasion to discuss the mentoring process with them. And you may be personally acquainted with mentees other than your own. Questions and discussions will naturally arise in a mentor-group setting, and some of these could contain uncomplimentary information about mentees. As a mentor, you must make two commitments at the very outset of the mentoring relationship and periodically reaffirm them:

● You will not identify the mentee who makes a statement or exhibits behavior that comes under discussion by a group of mentors.

● In cases where a slip is made or it is obvious who the mentee is, you will not pass the information along or make any mention of it to the mentee or anyone else—even as a lighthearted jest.

Many people can keep confidences that they know are important. Many of those same people, however, would mistakenly identify some pieces of information as unimportant. They might find it difficult, for instance, upon hearing some humorous or positive incident regarding a mentee they know well, to keep it to themselves. The temptation can be very strong to mention it in a teasingly innocent way or even as a compliment.

The difficulty is that the mentees immediately know the source of the information, and quickly discern that anything they say or do in the presence of their mentor might become public information. This significantly damages any trust in the relationship and undermines the integrity of the mentor in the eyes of the mentee.

If you have multiple mentees meeting together, you must encourage your mentees to adopt the same commitment toward each other. Although mentoring is neither purely counseling nor accountability, there are aspects of both involved. For the mentoring relationship to work at an optimal level, a sense of trust and mutual protection must be established early.

Be very careful about compromising confidentiality in the quest for prayer support. Some mentees may be experiencing difficulties that require diligent prayer from many people. An issue that is not already public knowledge must not become public knowledge as a result of your efforts to solicit prayer support. Sincere people of prayer are frequently called upon to do spiritual battle without knowing all the details or the identity of their subject. God knows and will reward both their efforts and their restraint in not requiring all the gory details.

Some kinds of information must be passed on to the appropriate people in a responsible way. Issues of abuse or behavior that could be seriously damaging to someone require something beyond confidentiality. Within a church setting, a pastor should determine what steps need to be taken. Once you have gone to a pastor with the issue, you must return to the confidentiality mode.

Evaluating Success

Gauging the success of a mentoring relationship isn't always easy. Defining expectations at the outset is a good start. Both sides of the relationship need to realize that successful mentoring can, and often does, occur without dramatic results. The same might be said of disciplines such as daily Bible reading and prayer. At the very least, we know the discipline is good for us. We can discern growth, but it's hard to see on a daily basis.

A person who journals can look back at entries a year earlier and see evidence of the maturing process. Measuring personal growth is like measuring the growth of a tree. Just watching it from day to day, you might think it's not growing at all, but a glance at the rings shows a steady annual increase.

Since life never gives us the opportunity to go down two paths simultaneously, we can never be certain of what would have happened if we had chosen a different track. Past experience leads us to believe, however, that there are some things we wouldn't have learned if we had not exposed ourselves to learning opportunities. Mentees should be able to look back on a year of mentoring and see character qualities and leadership skills they have developed.

A concept that is equally valid, but even more difficult to grasp, is the number of problems or even disasters we have avoided by virtue of the path we have chosen. We may not often think in these terms, but imagine the physical, spiritual, and emotional damage we avoid by simply obeying God's design for expressing our sexuality. A good accountability relationship provides some of this preventive benefit. Mentees should be able to look back on a year of mentoring and, without too much difficulty, imagine some of the mistakes they might have made in the absence of their mentoring experiences.

Keep in mind, however, that some individuals need considerable feedback in order to see evidence of their own growth. I recently asked a young man in my Sunday school class whether he could see growth in his life over the last year or two. He thought for a moment and said, "No, I don't think so."

I don't know him well, so I didn't press the issue in front of the class, but later I asked someone who does know him well. He couldn't believe the student's response. "Ask his parents," he said. "Ask anybody who knows him. There's been tremendous change and growth in his life!"

Some people—even some who behave very badly—have unrealistically high standards for themselves. Others may never have felt unconditionally loved and accepted (especially by their fathers) and feel that they can never measure up. No matter how much growth there might be, they have a perfectionist attitude that doesn't allow them to recognize improvement. The result for some is hostility and rebellion. For others it may be resignation or apathy. Positive, honest feedback from a mentor regarding even slight growth in a mentee can be a huge encouragement—one that unlocks the door to much greater and faster growth.

It's a good idea for you as a mentor to keep at least a simple journal of your own journeys. Encourage your mentees to do the same. One of the most valuable uses of a journal is to note small, private victories. It's the succession of these small, private victories that helps us build courage and faith, spurring us on to greater successes and public victories.

Both mentors and mentees must accept by faith that growth is virtually inherent in a mentoring relationship, even if it's slow and subtle. Pay close attention to the feedback your mentees give you. Sometimes it may be hard to discern, but they will probably express appreciation for your efforts in one way or another, letting you know that you're accomplishing something worthwhile.

Also, be sure to develop some measurable, attainable goals for your mentoring experience so that you can enjoy the sweet fulfillment of progress and accomplishment.

Some Things to Keep in Mind

Always keep in mind that you're doing a specialized kind of mentoring—one that combines a strong leadership emphasis with a discipleship thrust. General mentoring revolves around only two major questions for mentees:
- Where do you want to go?
- How can I help you get there?

Our specialized kind of mentoring doesn't abandon those questions. In fact, you'll want to make them a recurring theme. We add one additional consideration, however. It's summed up in this question for your mentees:
- Where should you go?

Ideally, the answers to this question will also come from the mentees, but you may need to give them considerable guidance to help them find the right answers. Many mentees, especially younger ones, aren't yet prepared to answer this question by themselves.

Your goal is not to usurp the role of the Holy Spirit in their lives, but to help them develop a vision and a hunger for God's plan for them. We know that God's plan for today's young people includes character development and the willingness to assume a degree of leadership, even if it's limited to their closest circles of influence. *Successful Youth Mentoring,* along with your own input and prayers, will help your mentees uncover God's plan and realize their potential.

You have the opportunity to play a pivotal role in the development of the young people you mentor. The privilege can be overwhelming, as can the responsibility. We urge you to rely on the riches of God's grace, which "he lavished on us with all wisdom and understanding" (Ephesians 1:8).

And we pray that God will "give you the Spirit of wisdom and revelation, so that you may know him better," and "that the eyes of your heart may be enlightened in order that you may know the hope to which he has called you, the riches of his glorious inheritance in the saints, and his incomparably great power for us who believe" (Ephesians 1:17b-19a).

Getting Started

Running the Risk

For Mentors Only

The sun is high, and excitement is so thick in the air you feel you could grab a handful and smear it on the sails. Crowds line the pier and stretch around the harbor as far as you can see. Most are cheering, laughing, celebrating—a few are crying. You are about to embark on a great adventure.

The rewards could be great, but the risk is enormous. Many of those cheering and celebrating are wishing they could go as well. They could, actually, if they had the courage.

There's plenty of room aboard these three ships sailing off to establish a new England. Can you feel the knot in your stomach as you try to imagine an unknown future? You could become a hero—or you could be dead at sea three days from now.

Part of the challenge of life is taking risks. A visionary must be willing to step out and boldly go where no one has gone before. Life in the harbor may be safe, but the greatest rewards lie in deep, uncharted waters.

The focus of this session is to help the mentees each take a risk in life as the Pilgrims did.

1. Introducing the Concept

◆ Option A: Share a personal risk experience.

Choose something from your student days…or something as recent as last week, when you summoned the courage to ask an important question in closing a huge sale. Maybe you confronted your boss with an issue that could cost your job. Tell what happened as vividly as possible. Include not only the circumstances but also the feelings. Re-create the tension—the urge to move ahead combined with the paralysis of fear. (Sharing your own vulnerability and emotions opens up a real opportunity to reveal character, which encourages your mentees.)

◆ Option B: Use this analogy.

People who fly planes are generally thought to be courageous. They have stepped out of the ordinary and put their lives in jeopardy beyond normal highway traffic.

Generally, though, they are not a foolhardy bunch. They constantly evaluate the risks. Before every flight they check the current weather as well as the forecast (both en route and at their destination) to make sure their plane and their piloting skills are up to the challenge. They then make a "go/no-go" decision based on that information.

They complete a thorough checklist of the plane's systems before entering the runway for takeoff. If something is not working as it should, they return for service. Even when they have begun their

takeoff run, they are constantly evaluating the plane's performance and progress. They eye a spot on the runway that represents another "go/no-go" decision. If they are not airborne by the time they reach that spot, they know they must abort the takeoff or else face the likelihood of not clearing obstacles ahead.

◆ Option C: Ask these questions.

- Can you recall a recent situation where someone you know acted with courage in taking a risk? Describe it.
- How about you? Tell me about a time when you had to make a "go/no-go" decision?
- How do you know when someone is being brave or being foolish—taking stupid risks?
- Have you ever heard the phrase "Wisdom is the better part of valor"? What does that mean to you?

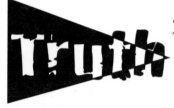

2. Truth Statement

There are worthy risks and foolish risks. Wisdom knows the difference, but fear avoids them all.

3. The Lesson

An acrostic on risk

This little memory device gives a framework for evaluating risk. You might want to scratch the outline down on a piece of paper as you present the concepts to your mentees.

Recognize the vision. Dream beyond average. Strive for excellence. Is this dream something that would please God? Is it in keeping with his character?

Interpret the risk. Seek counsel from experienced people whose judgment you trust. Is there a way to limit the risk? (Example: Go rock climbing or scuba diving after taking instruction, and make sure you have a partner.) Make sure the risk is reasonable and the reward is worthy.

Seize the day. Make a plan and step out in confidence. If you have planned carefully, move boldly. Too much hesitation can introduce self-defeating fear and doubt.

Know your limits. Sometimes unexpected things happen beyond your control. You may need to re-evaluate risk and cut losses. Always have a backup plan or escape route. The difference between bailing out too early and bailing out too late is often a fine line that requires wisdom and experience. Getting good counsel from the outset is very important. So is the attitude that says setbacks and failures are among the best learning tools.

Do a little self-check

We all have different natural responses to risk taking. Ask your mentees to answer these questions for themselves:

● Am I more likely to avoid risks or to take them on without reasonable consideration?

● Do I seek counsel from qualified people or just anyone at hand?

● Do I look for and listen to counsel that mostly agrees with what I want to do anyway, or do I deliberately seek opposing views?

● Do I learn from the past and avoid repeating the same mistakes?

● Do I understand that the outcome of a situation does not always prove whether a decision or risk was a good one? (POINT: We cannot control everything. Sometimes we may make the best choice based on the information available, and the result is still not to our liking. The opposite can also be true: We can make a foolhardy choice and get "lucky," at least this once!)

● What kind of adjustments could I make to improve my approach to risk?

Once the mentees have answered these questions for themselves, encourage them to get outside opinions on the same questions. Since we all have blind spots, it is often an eye-opener to ask someone else to respond, based on their view of the mentees.

You could volunteer to be the person they ask, unless they would be more comfortable asking someone else.

4. Ancient Wisdom

(The Scriptural Principle)

Many people throughout the Bible were excellent examples of visionary risk takers.

● Noah must have suffered great ridicule for building a ship on dry land because of the floods God had told him would come—and this was before there had ever been any rain. (Genesis 6-7)

● Abram (before God changed his name to Abraham) left his extended family and home when God told him to move far away to another land. He had no idea where he was going or how long it would take. He only knew God had promised to bless him and make him a father of nations. (Genesis 12:1-5)

● Joseph, Moses, Rahab, David, Ruth, Daniel, Esther, the prophets, the disciples, the apostles—all these and more showed courage in the face of the unknown. And it wasn't just that an unknown was forced on them. They chose to leave their comfort zones and risk great things in obedience to God.

A verse to remember
"I command you—be strong and courageous! Do not be afraid or discouraged. For the Lord your God is with you wherever you go" (Joshua 1:9 NLT).

5. The Closing

Life is full of risks. Intelligent people avoid foolish and unnecessary ones but plan and move with courage when the risk/reward ratio is favorable. They have appropriate confidence in
● the quality of the vision,
● their ability (and, in some cases, their team's ability), and

● God as their strength and source.

If we have faith in God, he will convince us that we can believe in ourselves and our abilities. That lets us move forward with confidence in any situation. Setbacks and failures become learning tools.

Something Extra

If you want to nail down this lesson even more, you might choose a particular risk situation—applying for a job, running for office at school, trying out for a sports team, mentioning the Lord in a conversation with an unchurched friend—and assign the mentees to think through the R-I-S-K approach. Next time you meet, ask for a report.

Folks Need Strokes

For Mentors Only

We live in an extraordinarily critical society. This is true for adults but even more so for teens. They face constant criticism, each teen being both a critic and a victim simultaneously. Parents easily fall into the trap of routinely criticizing their teens (it's not hard—they seem to supply us with plenty of good reasons). Brothers and sisters rip each other apart. Friends put subtle and not-so-subtle pressure on each other to conform to group norms. While Mom and Dad want to see good grades, the group applies more intense pressure not to get good grades.

Middle or junior high school is an especially tough war zone of insults, put-downs, back stabs, and smears, each warrior learning that the best defense is a good offense. Many do not survive well. Teens are pressured into smoking, drinking, and having sex. As a result they develop eating disorders and suicidal tendencies.

Home sometimes becomes even worse than school as the changes of adolescence rub raw wounds in familial relationships. Many kids seldom if ever hear a kind word, nor do they learn how to say anything decent about others.

You, as a mentor, will not change this world for your mentees. But you can have a significant influence by consciously deciding to encourage, compliment, affirm, and recognize good results. The purpose of this lesson is to learn the tools for affirmation.

Here are some general guidelines for you in your mentoring:

1. Be affirming, loving, accepting. Be careful not to use put-downs, even in jest.

2. Receive a compliment gracefully. Don't be shy; go ahead and give the correct answer, which is "Thank you."

3. Be specific in your compliments. General statements ("You are a cool person") are not as meaningful as specific statements ("I think it is really cool the way you help Sam with his math homework.")

4. Avoid complimenting things over which others have no control, for example, physical appearance or natural ability. "You have pretty eyes" is not as good as "Your eyes really sparkle when you laugh."

5. Avoid making comparisons, as in, "You are the smartest person in the tenth grade." Say rather, "I like your quick mind and how hard you work in your studies."

6. If younger teens seem self-conscious about giving affirmations, have them write them out first.

Condensed from *Building Community in Youth Groups*
(Loveland, CO: Group Publishing, 1985). Used by permission.

1. Introducing the Concept

◆ Option A: Share something from your life.

Tell a time when you were insulted or humiliated by a thoughtless comment. Tell also when someone gave you an unusually thoughtful compliment. Include the impact each event had on you.

◆ Option B: Use a newspaper attack.

Find an article, editorial, or letter to the editor that is particularly insulting, and discuss how you might feel if you were the brunt of that attack. Find also something that is complimentary (if you can), and talk about the impact it could have on your life if you were the target of the compliments.

◆ Option C: Use a personality feature.

Find a couple of magazine stories about famous people, such as sports figures, movie stars, computer whizzes, or someone else your mentees might find personally interesting. Choose one that raves about the person's talent or character, and another one that is critical. Talk for a minute about how the tone of each article would affect you if you were the subject.

2. Truth Statement

Encouragement accomplishes with joy what negative criticism can only attempt with pain.

3. The Lesson

Tape an episode of a TV show in which the characters insult each other. (It won't be hard to find—nearly every sitcom draws on one-liner insults as its primary source of humor.) Talk about the humor of the dialogue, and discuss the way each person in the show might actually react if it were a real-life situation.

Then talk about this issue of being humiliated:

● List some of the words and phrases used at school to cut people down.

● Describe a situation similar to the one in the TV show, when you have experienced embarrassment in front of friends, classmates, or teachers.

● Talk about a time when you saw someone else being insulted and embarrassed in front of people.

● Tell about a time when you disappointed friends, teachers, or parents.

Finally, turn the corner to practice the positive:

Active learning

◆ Option A: Write notes.

Each of you write an affirming note to a teacher, pastor, friend, or coworker. Review your notes together for positive comments and specific statements. Remember to avoid complimenting things over which others have no control (physical appearance or natural ability). Avoid making comparisons.

◆ **Option B: Affirm mentees.**

Affirm each mentee with a note you wrote prior to meeting. Point out two or three specific things you admire. After giving him or her an opportunity to read the note, ask how this makes the person feel. Uncomfortable? Encouraged? Talk about the proper way to receive a compliment.

◆ **Option C: Make lists.**

Allow two to three minutes for you and your mentees to write five things you like about yourselves. Read your lists to each other. Share with the others how you have seen those qualities exhibited.

4. Ancient Wisdom

(The Scriptural Principle)

In John 4:1-42, the Bible tells a story about Jesus meeting a woman at a well in the heat of the noonday sun. He knew that women always got their water for the day early in the morning, when it was still cool. It was also a social occasion when they would stand around and talk and laugh together.

He suspected that this woman was hiding from the rest of the women in town, and he knew why. She had had five husbands and was currently living with a man to whom she was not married. Her reputation was terrible, and people were no doubt constantly criticizing her for her bad choices.

But Jesus, rather than ripping her to shreds and telling her what a horrible person she was, did the unthinkable. He asked her for a drink of water. Then he spoke kindly to her even though she was a Samaritan—a group hated by the Jews in the same way that some people today hate others of different races. A Jew wouldn't normally speak to a Samaritan.

Rather than criticize her, he merely told her what he knew about her already and offered her "living water," the water of salvation. She was so excited when she realized that only the Messiah could have done these things. She ran to the rest of the town to tell them that he was here.

A kind and perceptive word from the Son of God changed not only her life, but the lives of many within the village.

A verse to remember
"Therefore encourage one another and build each other up" (1 Thessalonians 5:11).

5. The Closing

Work with your mentees to make a list of practical, creative ways to encourage others. For example, they might list things like writing poems for people on their birthdays, offering to help people who are overwhelmed with work, and planning surprise appreciation parties for no reason.

Remind your mentees that they represent Christ in the world. All of you accomplish that best by being encouragers rather than discouragers. Everyone needs someone to give a pat on the back.

Something Extra

Make a commitment to one another that you'll affirm at least ten people during the coming week. Keep a list of those affirmations.

Personality Strengths and Abilities

For Mentors Only

All people have personality strengths and weaknesses that impact their way of interacting with other people, their interests, and their personal and professional goals.

The four basic personality types have been given many labels over the years. In this lesson we'll use the following descriptions:

- Talkative/fun-loving
- Active/hard-driving
- Observer/easygoing
- Agreeable and organized

Although every person is likely to have a few qualities from each of the personality types, one category is usually prominent. Talking with your mentees about strengths and weaknesses in a constructive way will help strengthen their growth and maturity.

1. Introducing the Concept

◆ Option A: Talk about your families.

Spend some time talking about your family members and asking your mentees about their families. Ask everyone to describe the various personalities of their family members and to predict how their family members would act in the following scenarios:

- Your family has run across an unexpected opportunity to move to another town or city.
- Your family wins a contest, and the prize is an all-expenses-paid opportunity to redecorate your home.
- Your family decides to take a vacation together, and everyone gets to help plan it.

◆ Option B: Use an object lesson.

Place a transparent glass partially filled with water on a table. Ask your mentees to describe what they see.

After a few minutes, begin discussing how various people often describe the same object or experience in very different and unique ways. For instance, the four personality types would say:

- "The glass is half full." (Active/hard-driving)
- "The glass is half empty." (Agreeable and organized)
- "The glass is half full, no! Wait! Half empty! No, half…let me think about it." (Observer/easygoing)

● "It depends on how you look at it. Does it really matter?" (Talkative/fun-loving)

◆ Option C: Give some real-life illustrations.

Describe yourself and three or four individuals whom you believe are clear examples of the four types. Share the defining characteristics of these people.

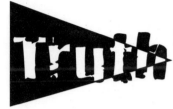

2. Truth Statement

Understanding what makes you and others tick is a key to great hidden potential.

3. The Lesson

Each of you should complete the following temperament assessment. Listed below are a number of personality strengths. Look them over and circle ten strengths that you think most apply to you.

Outgoing T	Personable T	Humorous O
Calm O	Efficient O	Decisive A
Gifted AO	Perfectionist AO	Warm T
Compassionate T	Talkative T	Dependable O
Loyal AO	Strong-Willed A	Independent A
Confident A	Enjoys Life T	Diplomatic O
Conservative O	Aesthetic AO	Practical A
Analytical AO	Carefree T	Leader A
Self-Sacrificing A	Determined A	Easygoing O
Productive O	Friendly T	Idealistic AO
Sensitive AO	Optimistic A	Enthusiastic T

Below is a list of personality weaknesses. Look them over and circle ten that you think most apply to you.

Restless T	Slow O	Impulsive T
Indecisive O	Loud T	Revengeful AO
Selfish O	Theoretical AO	Proud A
Inconsiderate A	Undisciplined T	Lazy O
Negative AO	Domineering A	Spectator O
Self-Protective O	Crafty A	Critical AO
Weak-Willed T	Self-Sufficient A	Exaggerates T
Stingy O	Self-Centered AO	Hot-Tempered A
Unmotivated O	Unemotional A	Fearful O
Undependable T	Teaser O	Unsociable AO
Impractical AO	Sarcastic A	Stubborn AO
Egotistical T	Rigid AO	Introspective AO
Depressive AO	Cruel A	Unstable T

Add the number of traits (both positive and negative) that correspond with each letter category ("T," "A," "O," and "AO").

Total number of "T" (Talkative) traits you circled: ____
Total number of "A" (Active) traits you circled: ____
Total number of "O" (Observer) traits you circled: ____
Total number of "AO" (Agreeable and Organized) traits you circled: ____

Here are a few ways the various personality types relate to career opportunities and also to friendships.

Talkative/Fun-Loving

On the Job
Quick to volunteer
Inspires others
Energetic
Enthusiastic
Quick starter

With Friends
Easy to befriend
Spontaneous/active
Gets excited
Loves interaction
Takes compliments

Active/Hard-Driving

On the Job
Practical
Quick to action
Sets goals
Organized
Enjoys opposition

With Friends
Organizes people
Cool in emergencies
Friendship is optional
Determined
Has a global outlook

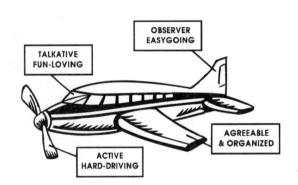

Observer/Easygoing

On the Job
Consistent
Avoids conflict
Seeks economy
Performs in spite of stress
Administrator

With Friends
Easygoing
Enjoyable
Has many friends
Compassionate
Good listener

Agreeable and Organized

On the Job
High expectations
Detail-oriented
Economical
Creative
Starts and finishes

With Friends
Cautious
Avoids attention
Seeks idealism
Devoted
Faithful

Now explore the implications of knowing your personality type. Ask:
- How do you think your personality type affects the way you interact with friends and family members every day?
- How can you increase your effectiveness in doing schoolwork and making career plans, now that you know more about your strengths and weaknesses?
- What might you do to increase your strengths and decrease your weaknesses?

4. Ancient Wisdom

(The Scriptural Principle)

Here is a biblical example of each personality type. Read the passage that describes someone most like you:
- Simon Peter (the talkative one)—Matthew 16:13-23; Luke 22:31-34
- Paul (the active one)—Acts 28:17-31
- Abraham (the observing one)—Genesis 12:1-9
- Moses (the agreeable and organized one)—Numbers 3:40-51

The most important aspect about personality is to learn how to use your strengths to best express the fruit of the Spirit as found in Galatians 5:22-23. This, in fact, is a good passage to memorize.

Verses to remember

"But the fruit of the Spirit is love, joy, peace, patience, kindness, goodness, faithfulness, gentleness and self-control. Against such things there is no law" (Galatians 5:22-23).

5. The Closing

If you are meeting in a public place, take a few minutes to observe people around you. Speculate about which of the four personality types you see.

Then talk about how your own strengths and weaknesses might affect how you look at others and how you interact with them.

Everyone has personality or temperament strengths and weaknesses that are an important part of who they are and what they do. Having identified your own personality type, you can become more effective in every area of your life.

However, resist the temptation to overemphasize your personality type or label. This might result in missing some potential talents and abilities yet to be discovered as you grow and mature in the years ahead.

Making the Right Decisions for the Right Reasons

For Mentors Only

Daniel (of lion's den fame), Joan of Arc, William Wilberforce, Abraham Lincoln, Martin Luther King, Rosa Parks—these were men and women who saw the direction the parade was going and chose to help turn it around. History is full of people—some famous, some unknown—who were willing to stand for right in the face of scorn, adversity, and danger. That meant moving against the flow; refusing to bow to peer pressure. Their integrity wouldn't let them do it any other way.

That commitment is necessary in order to be a person of influence and impact. It is a lifestyle that must be nourished in routine activities so a person is ready when major decision moments come.

1. Introducing the Concept

Begin with a story

◆ Option A: Tell an embarrassing story.

Talk about an embarrassing fad or fashion (bell bottoms, pet rocks) you once adopted just to go along with others. If you have a visual reminder—pictures, an item, scrapbook—bring it along. Ask your mentees what they think might some day be one of their silly fads or fashions.

◆ Option B: Share your experience.

Tell about a time you made the right decision to stand up for something...or the wrong decision to just go along with the crowd.

◆ Option C: Tell this story from the author's life.

In college I joined a prank pulled on a blind student. While someone engaged Bob in conversation, others silently surrounded him with a barricade of student-center furniture. When it was time for him to leave, his cane hit unfamiliar obstacles in every direction. I stood with the others and watched his frustration. None of us said, "This is wrong," nor did we go to assist Bob. Instead, we meekly let the prank run its course.

Interact with your mentees about why it is easy to go along with the flow even when it's going the wrong way.

Hear their stories

Say something like, "Tell me about a time you felt good about standing up for something" or "Tell me about a time you made the right decision in a tough situation." Listen closely for follow-up interaction opportunities.

Take a field trip

◆ Option A: Visit a historical site.

Visit a historical site that illustrates the concept of making a decision to do the right thing. Investigate the background story to help you make application. Or perhaps the site shows people not making the right decision.

◆ Option B: Visit a person.

Visit a person whose life ties in directly with the lesson—someone who took a strong stand for truth, or someone who suffered because no one was willing to make the right decision.

What if...

Create a scenario that raises the issue of choosing to do the right thing, such as:

● Suppose you went to a party with some friends and they decided to start drinking...How would you respond?

● Suppose you discovered that a friend who works with you is stealing from the company, and he wants to let you in on his "action." ...How would you decide what to do?

2. Truth Statement

Right is right even if no one is doing it. Wrong is wrong even if everyone is doing it.

Follow up with these questions:

● What makes most people go along with the crowd?

● How is it that some people are willing to make right decisions when there is enormous pressure all around to do the opposite?

● What are major barriers to living this way?

● What advice would you give a friend to help him or her move past those barriers?

3. The Lesson

Here are five simple steps toward standing for right when those around you are doing wrong.

1. Set standards and be guided by them. Football wouldn't be the same without a goal line to aim for. Basketball wouldn't be the same without a hoop. Living without standards creates a similar lack of direction. If you

determine what kind of person you will be and what you believe, it's easier to make the right decision when pressure comes.

2. Think about the consequences of your decisions before you act. How will you (and others) be affected? What might the long-term results be?

3. Actions don't have to follow feelings. I may feel like eating a dozen of those freshly baked chocolate chip cookies. However, I have set certain healthy eating standards. I think about the consequences and limit my actions to two cookies. You may feel outside pressure or even your own desire to make a wrong decision, but you don't have to act on those feelings. You probably don't feel like doing homework, but since you set a certain academic goal, you do it anyway.

4. Be aware of negative influences in your life. Do certain people, places, or things encourage you to make wrong decisions? Don't stand around and let a snake bite you. Either destroy the threat or get away from it.

5. Develop a life habit of doing the right thing, not just the easy thing. The easy thing may not be wrong, but it may not be best.

You can develop these ideas with your mentees using visual aids: a map for guidance, a picture of a mountain, a cookie, a drawing of a football field on a napkin, and so on.

You could also walk around, discussing steps as you actually take physical steps.

Or perhaps you'd like to talk while doing an activity together, such as shooting baskets or making cookies.

4. Ancient Wisdom

(The Scriptural Principle)

The 37th chapter of Genesis begins the remarkable story of Joseph—you remember, the guy with the amazing Technicolor dreamcoat. Joseph's brothers were so filled with jealousy and rage over his arrogance and the preferential treatment he got from his father, they decided to murder him and disguise it as an accident.

Reuben, one of the brothers, intervened and came up with an alternate plan in order to spare Joseph's life. Given the emotional state of the other brothers and their obvious willingness to kill, you can imagine the courage it must have taken for Reuben to confront them and try to stop their plan. They could have killed him as well. But he knew their plan was wrong, in spite of all Joseph had said and done to incite them—and in spite of the possibility that Joseph's dreams might come true and they would all be ruled by him.

So Reuben turned the parade around. He did the right thing for the right reason. You know the rest of the story, but even if it hadn't turned out for their benefit in the end, he was still right to do the right thing for the right reason. Whether anyone else realized it or not, he knew it and God knew it. Nothing is different today.

Verses to remember

"Be on your guard; stand firm in the faith; be men [and women] of courage; be strong. Do everything in love" (1 Corinthians 16:13-14).

5. The Closing

E. B. White wrote, "As long as there is one upright man, as long as there is one compassionate woman, the contagion may spread and the scene is not desolate."

With your mentees, evaluate your lives by asking, "Am I going along with something I don't feel right about?" If the answer is yes, decide to do something positive to change.

Life's Greatest Adventure

Conviction

For Mentors Only

At the core of every successful person's life are the deep convictions out of which he or she operates. Living life's greatest adventure begins with the conviction that there is a God and that he wants to be personally involved in our lives.

Christians are convinced that apart from this personal relationship with God, life has no ultimate meaning. We were created to have fellowship with God. Without that fellowship there is a great vacuum; an emptiness that produces a life of selfishness and separation from God.

Before we go any further in mentoring, we need to make sure that each of your mentees has decided to accept God's forgiveness of sin and has invited him inside.

1. Introducing the Concept

◆ Option A: Make a list.

Ask your mentees to write a list of the most important things in life. Give plenty of time, and don't limit the list in any way.

Also, don't worry if the answers are not too "spiritual."

◆ Option B: Tell your story.

Describe the personal trail by which you became a Christian. If you have never done this before, try following these simple steps:

1. Give some background: Where were you? What was your life like before you invited Christ to be your Savior? What made you realize you needed God in your life?

2. Tell the circumstances of your conversion. For example, did a friend talk to you about receiving Christ into your life? Perhaps you made the decision at church or at an evangelistic rally, or you responded to an invitation you heard on television, or maybe you were simply reading the Bible and felt a need to respond.

3. Tell exactly what you did to respond to the claims of Christ, for example: "I decided right there that I needed to make a commitment to Jesus, so I bowed my head and prayed."

4. Talk briefly about the difference that decision has made in your life, for example: "Since receiving Jesus into my life, I've changed in the following ways..."

◆ Option C: Hear someone else's story.

Invite a Christian friend to share about how he or she received God's gift of forgiveness by believing in Jesus. Set it up with your friend ahead of time. Choose someone both you and your mentees hold in high regard—someone who is accustomed to sharing a personal story of faith.

2. Truth Statement

Guilt is a given. We can have the gift of peace with God—if we will accept it.

3. The Lesson

Hint: If any of your mentees have not yet made a commitment to Christ, this is the week that will highlight this step as never before. If your mentees have made a commitment to Jesus, go ahead and use this material anyway by saying, "Let's review how to make the Gospel crystal-clear to your non-Christian friends. You've no doubt heard more than a few calls to tell others about Christ, and you've wondered inside just what you would say if the opportunity ever came along. OK—here's the core of how you share your faith with others."

For this lesson we suggest that you open this mentor's guide and go through the following material with the mentees looking on. Try not to get sidetracked by additional explanations—especially long and involved ones. Instead, offer to come back, if necessary, to a particular point and discuss it after finishing the presentation. This allows God's Spirit to work in an individual's heart, and often makes earlier objections irrelevant.

You need to know that God loves you and wants a personal relationship with you.

"For God so loved the world that he gave his one and only Son, that whoever believes in him shall not perish but have eternal life" (John 3:16).

God wants you to know him personally. (John 17:3)

God created you and is excited about you! (Psalm 139:13-14)

Why is it that many people do not have a personal relationship with God?

You need to understand that your sin keeps you from having a personal relationship with God.

"For all have sinned and fall short of the glory of God" (Romans 3:23).

What is sin? (James 4:17)

Sin means doing wrong or failing to do all that God wants.

Sin is also your selfish attitude of ignoring or rejecting God.

What happens when you sin? (Isaiah 59:2; Romans 6:23)

Your sin causes a gap between God and you. The penalty for your sin is death, which means eternal separation from God.

What is the solution to your separation from God?

You need to know that Jesus Christ died and rose again so that your sins could be forgiven.

"For Christ died for sins once for all, the righteous for the unrighteous, to bring you to God" (1 Peter 3:18).

Jesus Christ

…died to pay the penalty for your sins. (Romans 5:8)

...rose again, which proves he can forgive you. (1 Corinthians 15:3-6)

...bridges the gap between God and you. (1 Timothy 2:5)

...is the only way to a relationship with God. (John 14:6)

 How can you begin your personal relationship with God?

You need to understand that you must personally trust Jesus Christ to be your Savior.

"Yet to all who received him, to those who believed in his name, he gave the right to become children of God" (John 1:12).

Trusting Jesus Christ means

...you turn to God from your own way of living. (Acts 3:19)

...you receive God's gift of salvation. (Ephesians 2:8-9)

A relationship with Jesus is not something you can earn. It is not just an emotional experience, nor is it just agreeing in your mind that Jesus is the Son of God. It is an act of your will and means total trust.

 So here's the question...

Are you ready for a personal relationship with God?

Which of these three sentences fits you?

"I don't have a personal relationship with God."

"I would like a personal relationship with God."

"I have a personal relationship with God."

You can begin your personal relationship with God by simply expressing yourself to God through prayer. Here's an example:

"Dear God, I know that my sin has separated me from you. Thank you that Jesus Christ died in my place and rose again to be my Savior. I turn from my sin and trust Jesus to forgive me. Come into my life and lead me. Thank you for giving me a relationship with you forever. In Jesus' name, Amen."

If you're ready to respond to God, pray right now and trust Jesus to forgive your sins and come into your life.

 What's next?

You should know that your trust in Jesus Christ begins a lifelong relationship.

God is never absent. "God has said, 'Never will I leave you; never will I forsake you'" (Hebrews 13:5).

God completely forgives your sin. "He forgave us all our sins, having canceled the written code, with its regulations, that was against us and that stood opposed to us" (Colossians 2:13-14).

God guarantees that you'll go to heaven. "I write these things to you who believe in the name of the Son of God so that you may know that you have eternal life" (1 John 5:13).

God gives you the Holy Spirit to enable you to live the Christian life. "Since we live by the Spirit, let us keep in step with the Spirit" (Galatians 5:25).

 What should you remember?

You can depend on God and his Word as you go through life's greatest adventure.

Now that you have made a commitment to Jesus, you must realize that

God will always be committed to you. His Word, the Bible, is completely true. Trust God's promises!

Because life is full of ups and downs, you must rely on the factual promises of God's Word, not on your feelings. Good feelings will come and go, but the fact that God loves you, forgives you, and promises eternal life in heaven will never change.

You have trusted Jesus Christ as your Savior—now let Jesus Christ be your LORD…

Learn everything you can about Jesus Christ. (2 Peter 3:18)
Study the Bible
Pray
Get involved in church
Obey God in every area of your life. (John 14:15)
He knows what's best for you!
Rely on God's Holy Spirit. (Galatians 5:16-17)
He will lead and guide you.
Decide to be like Jesus Christ. (Colossians 3:10)
This is the purpose of our great adventure called *life.*

The above material is taken from "Life's Greatest Adventure" and is copyrighted by Youth for Christ/USA. Gratefully used by permission.

4. Ancient Wisdom
(The Scriptural Principle)

In John 3:1-21 the Bible tells of a man named Nicodemus, who was on the Jewish ruling council. He met Jesus one night and acknowledged that Jesus was a teacher from God because, as he said, "No one could perform the miraculous signs you are doing if God were not with him."

Jesus more or less brushed right past the compliment, going on to explain that no one could get into the kingdom of God unless he was born again. Well, you can imagine where this conversation went…but the end result was Jesus' explanation that being "born again" is what happens whenever someone believes in him and receives eternal life.

Here's the most important thing Jesus said that night:

A verse to remember
"For God so loved the world that he gave his one and only Son, that whoever believes in him shall not perish but have eternal life" (John 3:16).

5. The Closing

Explain again to your mentees that making this decision starts us on the road of Life's Greatest Adventure. Explain that God will help us to:
1. Live a Christ-centered life.
2. Share our faith with others.
3. Be the kind of person God wants.

Series 1

Something Extra

If one or more of your mentees made the decision to invite Jesus into his or her life during this session, agree together that you will share this wonderful news with three people who care (mother, father, grandparent, pastor, Sunday school teacher, or friend).

Review, Reflect, and Respond

For Mentors Only

The last session of each six-week series is designed to be a review of the entire series. You will look at specific concepts that you and your mentees should have learned. If you find some things that are still unclear to you, go over the material of that lesson again.

The purpose of this lesson is to reinforce what you have studied together and to make sure you are beginning to put these concepts into practice.

1. The Truth Statements

During the past five weeks we have discussed the following concepts:

There are worthy risks and foolish risks. Wisdom knows the difference, but fear avoids them all.

Encouragement accomplishes with joy what negative criticism can only attempt with pain.

Understanding what makes you and others tick is a key to great hidden potential.

Right is right even if no one is doing it. Wrong is wrong even if everyone is doing it.

Guilt is a given. We can have the gift of peace with God—if we will accept it.

Review each of these truth statements from the previous lessons with your mentees. Consider the following questions:

● What makes each of these statements important?
● How are these concepts beginning to impact your life?

2. Review

In the first lesson of this series ("Running the Risk"), we used an acrostic to show the courage it takes to be a success in life. RISK means to:

Recognize the vision.
Interpret the risk.
Seize the day.
Know your limits.

We learned to avoid foolish and unnecessary risks, but also to plan and move with courage when the risk/reward ratio is favorable. This is based on confidence in the quality of the vision, our ability and/or that of our team, and God as our strength and source

The second lesson ("Folks Need Strokes") taught us to build others up rather than tear them down; to encourage rather than discourage. Learning to affirm and encourage is a necessary lesson for any aspiring leader.

One of the lesson options suggested that you each write a note to someone, affirming them for what they do. Did you do this exercise? If so, what was the result? Did you hear back from that person?

Get into the habit of looking for ways to compliment the people around you, always with sincerity.

The third lesson ("Personality Strengths and Abilities") was designed to help you uncover the strengths and weaknesses of your temperament. Do you think you understand yourself better after taking the test?

People react differently to the same situation because they are made differently. Knowing your temperament traits and learning to observe and understand others will result in:

● Knowing how to resolve conflicts with others;

● Understanding why someone may overreact to one situation but not another;

● Knowing why certain people are always the life of the party while others never speak unless they are asked a question.

What is your dominant temperament trait?

Make a list of some friends and discuss what you think their temperaments are, based on what you know now.

In the fourth week ("Making the Right Decisions for the Right Reasons") you learned the importance of taking a stand to do the right thing when there is a lot of pressure to do otherwise. Just like swimming against a current, taking a stand for what is right is hard. But when you reach your goal, the satisfaction is overwhelming.

Integrity is doing what is right. In the long run, the dividends for doing right are far greater than those for doing what is convenient or easy.

List some times when you have stood alone because it was the right thing to do.

Last week we focused on "Life's Greatest Adventure." Inviting Jesus Christ into your heart and life is the most important decision you'll ever make. It not only affects where you spend eternity, but it also sets you on a course for serving Christ.

If you have made that decision to follow Jesus Christ as your Lord and Savior, let's stop right now to thank him for coming into your heart. Restate your commitment to follow him faithfully.

3. The Closing

Now it's time to make a decision. We hope you have had a good time with this first series of lessons and that you learned a lot. But now you must decide whether to go on with the mentoring process.

If you all—mentor and mentees—make a commitment to continue, seal it with a handshake or a hug. Then agree to take a little time off, and set a date when you will begin the second series.

You Want Me to Do What?

Courage

For Mentors Only

This lesson is about learning to be accountable—a secret to achievement in life. Accountability helps us do the things we need to do in order to get to the place we want to be. So long as your mentees don't have to face up to their track records, the view is cloudy. But reaching goals and seeing dreams come true is usually the fruit of being accountable for your actions. And that requires courage.

1. Introducing the Concept

◆ Option A: Tell a one-sentence joke.

Introduce the difference between starting and carrying through by saying, "Did you hear the one about the kamikaze pilot who flew fifty missions?"

(You'll have to pause until your audience gets it. If they blank out on you, define a kamikaze pilot: a person in World War II who made the great commitment to dive his plane into an enemy ship, thus blowing it up—but also sacrificing his life. Any such pilot who flew fifty missions must have chickened out the first forty-nine times…)

Then say something like, "Accountability is a way to make sure we follow through on our dreams and ideas. It is getting someone to periodically check on us to make sure we did what we said we'd do. Without accountability, it is too easy to become big talkers and big dreamers who never actually do much."

◆ Option B: Tell your own story.

If you've had some personal experiences in accountability, describe them. Start by saying, "I want to tell you one of the big secrets to getting things done in my life." Then sketch out the background scene, describe the characters, and begin adding the dialogue in a compelling way, almost like a movie maker.

Maybe somewhere in your life, someone older or wiser than you took you under wing and held you accountable to actually do what you were talking and dreaming about. Or maybe you've been in a small group that held each other accountable. Describe the people, tell how it worked, and how it strengthened you as a leader and a Christian.

After your mentees hear your story, they will hopefully hunger for such a relationship themselves.

◆ Option C: Make a list.

Either verbally or on a place mat or sheet of scrap paper, help your mentees make lists of "things I'd like to do in my lifetime." Teenagers often have dreams and hidden goals they've never verbalized, let alone written down. Items might include sky diving, having a certain kind of car, getting a college degree, having a family, going some place interesting for vacation, taking a great canoe trip, whatever—the worthiness is not so important as building a list that illustrates how we all have dreams and hopes.

Once the list is written, point out that it is often easier to hope or dream than actually to accomplish these hopes and dreams. What is the secret to turning dreams and hopes into reality?

2. Truth Statement

Inch by inch anything's a cinch, but what we often lack is help to stay on track.

3. The Lesson

◆ Option A: Go rock climbing.

Take your mentees rock climbing, either outdoors or at an indoor climbing center. If you're unfamiliar with this sport, be sure to have a trained instructor help you. After the adventure, talk with your mentees about the experience and what it meant to have others there to help them make the climb.

◆ Option B: Tell a success story.

Recall some goal you set (or spiritual characteristic you wanted to develop) and how you accomplished it by breaking it down into smaller steps. Tell how someone held you accountable to make sure you did the smaller steps…If you've never done this, try the next option!

◆ Option C: Tell a failure story.

Only fools learn from success alone; wise people learn as much from failure—their own and the failures of others. If you had a great dream once, but never took the little steps toward accomplishing it, you probably wish you had the chance to do it again. By honestly sharing the story of how you passed the exit and missed out on accomplishment, you might make the point in an even stronger way.

◆ Option D: Use an object lesson.

Bring a short section of rope and have your mentees unravel it, illustrating the strength of intertwined cords, often three of them. This demonstrates how accountability with one person is good, but accountability with two people is even better.

Ask: "Besides being accountable to me for your goals, who else might be a good partner for you? Setting up accountability is a skill you can use all your life, so start thinking now of someone who could hold you accountable besides me."

Start with big goals

"Let's both write out two goals we want to accomplish within the year—one a general goal (for example, get a certain grade this quarter or semester, get my antique car finished) and the second one a spiritual goal (such as read the whole New Testament this year, or go on a missions trip)." Take time to write out the goals and then share them with each other.

Then analyze the small steps

Now, each of you break down both goals into smaller steps. For instance, getting a better grade requires a dozen specific actions involving note taking and studying. (HINT: This may force you to revise the overall goal. Many of us call something a goal when it is really just a hope—that is, we are not really willing to pay the "small steps" price to get it. If the small steps make you lose heart, then change your attitude or change the goal; you are not serious about it.)

Once you have listed the smaller steps toward the big goal, circle the first three steps you'll need to take. Make two copies and agree to hold each other accountable during your next time together for taking these first steps toward the goal.

4. Ancient Wisdom

(The Scriptural Principle)

After the twelve disciples had been with Jesus for a year or so, he sent them out to do the same things he had been doing. (See the record in Mark 6:7-13, 30 or Luke 9:1-6, 10.)

It has been a principle from the beginning of time that the first stage of learning something is to watch a master work. The second stage is to help the master work. The third is to work together with the master. Finally a day comes when the master sends the apprentices or mentees out to do the work themselves.

Jesus followed this principle when he sent the disciples out with instructions to heal others and preach as he had shown them during the last year or so. However, he did not turn them loose at this point without accountability. They were to return and report what they had done and get further training.

A verse to remember

"Though one may be overpowered, two can defend themselves. A cord of three strands is not quickly broken" (Ecclesiastes 4:12).

5. The Closing

You have both agreed to do several things before you meet again, and to hold each other accountable for them. However, the hardest steps are often the first one and the last one. Many great plans get sidelined when they are not yet started or when they are 90 percent finished. For now, the final step is not a worry—but the first step is. Go to work on your first single step of a long journey.

What we've learned

Successful people are more than dreamers who have big ideas; they break those big projects down into small steps. Then they set up accountability to make sure they actually take the small steps toward accomplishing their great dream.

Something Extra

Try to find something tangible to serve as a reminder of the first small step you both have to take. It might be a marble you carry in your pocket, a little object you hang from the mirror in your car, something to display on the bedroom door, or a simple pebble you pick up from a parking lot and slip into your pocket. These will remind you both that other person will be holding you accountable next week!

It's Your Serve

Compassion *(vertical text, right margin)*

For Mentors Only

Authentic leaders are servant leaders. They are men and women who demonstrate that they live to improve the lives of others rather than to pamper themselves. They are not easily distracted from the needs of others by possessions, prestige, popularity, or positions. They live with simple conviction—a conviction to bring light to the world by serving others. By leading through a lifestyle of servanthood, they make a deep impact on their world.

The focus of this time together is developing a lifestyle of serving others. You and your mentees will think out and put into action the concept of being a light to the world by serving people.

Checkup

Find out how your mentees did at taking the first steps toward the goal as outlined last week. Encourage and compliment...or else do a little prodding, as needed!

Before you go on, give your own progress report. How well did you do at taking your first steps?

1. Introducing the Concept

◆ Option A: Go out to eat.

Go to breakfast (or go for a late-night snack just to be different). But before you eat, spend a few minutes simply serving. Hold the door open for some other customers. Pick up some trash in the parking lot. Clean off some tables. Let someone else get in line ahead of you.

◆ Option B: Pick up garbage.

Take a plastic bag and spend thirty minutes to an hour picking up trash in a park, along a street, or on a playground. Success is not arriving at a position where you can hire someone else to pick up your garbage. It is helping the world pick up its garbage. Discuss this contrast with your mentees as you serve together.

◆ Option C: Take a field trip.

Go to a place of service or to a person in need. For example, visit an emergency room at a hospital, a rescue mission at mealtime, or a busy cafeteria. Sit and observe for thirty to sixty minutes. Notice needs being met or ignored. Notice people who go the extra mile to serve and those who get involved only out of obligation. Notice the attitudes of servers and those served.

While doing one or more of these options, look for chances to focus on being a light by serving. Tell a story about a time you were served and how it impacted your life, or a story about a time you experienced the joy of serving others. Ask questions such as these:

"What have you noticed about...?"

"How did you feel while we were...?"

"What are you thinking while picking up garbage?"

Tell about the historic Scotsman William Wallace, who addressed the ruling class of his country with this remark, "You think the people of this country exist to provide you with position. I think your position exists to provide those people with freedom, and I go to make sure that they have it."

2. Truth Statement

The path of true greatness is hidden in the camouflage of humble service.

3. The Lesson

A lifestyle committed to serving others is what separates authentic leaders from those who merely seek positions or glory. It is important for you to help your mentees internalize that concept. Although the introduction (Point 1) has already provided the bulk of this session, don't overlook driving the lesson home.

Ask one or more of these questions:

● Why do you think some people live to serve others rather than live to look after only their own interests?

● Why are some people willing to sacrifice relationships for the sake of having a few more things or a bit more prestige?

● How would you feel if someone gave $50 in your name to a homeless shelter rather than giving you two tickets to your favorite concert? Why?

● What are some things that squeeze out the importance of people and serving them? What makes these things seem to be more important than people?

Let the questions sink in. Give time for reflection. Stretch your mentees to develop a list of answers for the questions.

Use a visual aid

Bring a light bulb and a marker to write on it, or draw a light bulb with five shafts of light emanating from it. Quickly work through the following five hints on being a light. Write them on the bulb or on the five shafts of light.

1. Look for opportunities to serve. (Talk about opportunities both you and your mentees have.)

2. Involvement is a choice. (There's a big distance between seeing opportunities and actually doing something. What steps must be taken to get involved?)

3. Give for the sake of giving, not getting. (Stress the fact that servanthood is not favor-seeking—for example, mowing the lawn in order to get the car keys.)

4. Help doesn't need to be complicated. (Most acts of serving are simple: visiting the lonely, sharing time, giving a glass of cold water on a hot day, running an errand.)

5. Target others, not self.

4. Ancient Wisdom

(The Scriptural Principle)

Jesus Christ's life constantly demonstrated the question "How can I help you?" Not only did he say, "Even the Son of Man did not come to be served, but to serve" (Mark 10:45), but he showed it. Giving food to the hungry, sight to the blind, time to children, his life for us...Jesus constantly served others. Through his serving he was light to a dark world.

An Old Testament king named Rehoboam got some wise advice in 2 Chronicles 10:7. He chose not to follow it—and that choice hurt him at the time. The advice was, "If you will be kind to these people and please them and give them a favorable answer, they will always be your servants." People are naturally drawn to those willing to take a humble position.

A verse to remember
"Even the Son of Man did not come to be served, but to serve." (Mark 10:45)

5. The Closing

Agree with your mentees to practice improving people's moments. It's a simple concept: Do what you can to make the "right now" better for people. It might be raking leaves, holding a door open, offering an encouraging word, writing a note, or volunteering with a service organization. It's a matter of keeping your eyes and heart open to the people around you.

Over the next week, keep track of the things you do for others—and how it affects you. The next time you meet, discuss the results.

Close this session by giving each of your mentees a small towel or cloth napkin, symbolic of the towel Jesus used when he washed the disciples' feet (see John 13:4-5). Have each young person hang it in a prominent place as a daily reminder that authentic living is seen in the desire and action of serving others.

Something Extra

Together, organize and work on a project that reinforces the concept of serving others. For example:
● Have a garage sale and give the proceeds to an organization that is serving others and meeting needs. Don't just sell hand-me-downs and leftovers—put out some treasures as well.
● Collect goods for a mission or crisis center. Don't just clear out the cupboards (pork and beans), but donate things that would be a special treat to receive.

It's Your Serve

Developing a Life Mission Statement

For Mentors Only

What would you say is your life mission? Have you ever prepared a Life Mission Statement? To most people it sounds a little intimidating, maybe even presumptuous. Relax—this session is not so much about conjuring up an eloquent statement as it is about uncovering God's purpose already inside you and your mentees.

1. Introducing the Concept

◆ Option A: Tell a story.

The Nobel Peace Prize is given each year to someone who has done the most for world peace. What your mentees may not know is that Alfred Nobel also invented dynamite. He was the first to harness the power of nitroglycerin.

One morning Nobel opened his newspaper and read his own obituary! Somehow the press had confused the death of another man with him and printed the story of Nobel's life instead. He read that his greatest achievement was the invention of dynamite. The obituary went into some detail about how dynamite had changed the nature of warfare, increasing the efficiency and scope of killing.

Nobel was horrified to think that this was his legacy to the world. He had become wealthy making and selling dynamite for armies to slaughter each other. But now he had the rare opportunity to change his legacy—his life mission. He resolved to leave a different memory of himself and endowed the Nobel Peace Prize with his own fortune.

Today his name is synonymous with peace and the pursuit of knowledge. Hardly anyone remembers him as the inventor of dynamite.

◆ Option B: Use your imagination.

This game may sound a bit macabre in the beginning, but it can be extremely helpful in getting young minds geared up to think through a Life Mission Statement.

Imagine what it would be like if you could actually attend your own funeral. You slip into the church and sit in the back. No one notices you. As you listen to what people are saying about you in their eulogies, you realize what you have actually accomplished in their eyes. Imagine what you are hearing…

● What common themes keep coming up?
● What do people seem to think your life mission was?
● Is it anything like what you had in mind—what you intended your life to be about?

This memorial service gives me the opportunity to share some things I should have said years ago…

2. Truth Statement

Mission is purpose coupled with passion, unlocking power to pursue God's plan.

3. The Lesson

◆ Option A: Discuss these questions:

● Have you had days when you had lots of energy and got many things accomplished? Describe one of them.

● Have you also had days when you felt drained of energy and seemed to get nothing done? Again, describe.

● Have you ever wondered what the difference was?

Many factors can explain this, but one of the greatest is the difference in the sense of purpose and clear objectives we possessed at the time.

◆ Option B: Discuss briefly:

● Can you name some people you know today who have a clear purpose?

● Or can you name some biblical characters who definitely had a clear purpose? Look up Philippians 3:10-14. From this passage, how do you think Paul's mission statement might have read?

◆ Option C: Tell your own story.

Take a few minutes and share how you have attempted to sort out your mission in life. Be vulnerable; reveal your struggles, your doubts along the way, and what your understanding is now.

Thinking it through

Now proceed to *put something on paper*. Here are some insights that will make the task a little easier. Have your mentees take out a pad of paper and start writing notes.

1. **Your mission should start with yourself.**

Your mission statement will be unique, because you are unique. Write down your responses to the items on this list:

● Your talents and gifts—What do you do well?
● Your desire and passion—What do you really want to do in life?
● Your affirmation and recognition—What do others say you do well?
● Your fulfillment and satisfaction—What do you deeply enjoy?

2. **Your mission should include life-changing convictions.**

Your statement of purpose should contain ideas, dreams, and convictions that direct the course of your life. They should either reflect the values you already embrace or the ones you want to become a part of your life. Examples might be:

● Choosing to love God with all of your heart, mind, soul and strength
● Loving your neighbor as yourself
● Sharing your faith with others
● Spending a significant part of your energy and resources serving others

● Praying for people in need

3. Your mission should include others.

Notice how many of the above examples relate to other people. Your mission statement, if it is a biblical one, will always be centered around others. Jesus never calls anyone to a lone-ranger lifestyle that does not involve serving other people and enabling them to experience God's truth and love.

Remember: What we do for ourselves alone—dies with us. What we do for others and the world remains forever. The legacy you leave will be determined by what you do to serve humanity. The mature Christian is one whose lifestyle revolves around ministry to other people, beginning with those in one's own family.

Consider the answers to these questions:

● What are my greatest burdens? What human needs make me angry or make me cry?

● What resources do I possess that I could use to serve others? What could I give away? Do I have a generous spirit when it comes to my talents and time?

● Do I really love others? Does my agenda significantly include the needs of others?

4. Your mission should be big.

A mission statement should require a lifetime to fulfill as well as God's power to pull off. Your purpose should not be something that can be accomplished in a couple of years. Richard Bach has a simple test to determine whether one's mission in life is accomplished: "If you are alive, it isn't."

Consider the answers to these questions:

● If you had no fear of failure, what would you attempt to do?

● Remember the earlier exercise of attending your own funeral? What would you want people to be saying about you? Looking back on your life from the other end, what kinds of accomplishments and character would you like to see?

5. Your mission should have eternal value.

Consider the answers to these questions:

● What do you believe Jesus meant when he said, "Do not store up for yourselves treasures on earth…but store up for yourselves treasures in heaven" (Matthew 6:19-20). Do you have a personal application you could make for this Scripture?

● What do you believe God values most, based on your knowledge of him?

● How could you impact the world for eternity, using your God-given abilities?

6. Your mission should be based on God's priorities.

God's priorities can be summed up with the Great Commandment and the Great Commission: To love the Lord with all your heart, to love your neighbor as yourself, and to go make disciples of all nations.

An even shorter version of this is the phrase: "To know him and to make him known."

Make sure your mentees know they are not being pressured to enter full-time ministry as a career. Although much of the preceding has had a strong Christian service emphasis, it does not imply that all dedicated Christians should be professional church workers. God blesses and empowers people in nearly any profession if their desire is to be diligent and work as if working for God.

Writing the statement

You will have to determine the maturity level of your mentees and how much help to give them with this part. A Life Mission Statement doesn't have to be more than a couple of sentences. Here's an example of one for a young man; it's generic with regard to vocation and family, since those choices were not yet made:

"My life mission is to seek and wholeheartedly follow God's leading in every part of my life. I will diligently continue my education so that I will be prepared to excel in my field of service. If and when I have a family, I will take the responsibility to serve them as a godly husband and father, making their total welfare a priority over career, outside interests, and even other forms of ministry."

Important hints

● Don't just adopt the above sample. Your statement must be your statement. It's better to have something plain that you have created from your own heart and mind than something fancy that you borrowed.

● If your mentees have a strong leading as to vocation, they might include how they see pursuing it with a unique sense of excellence for Christ. Other things that are important to them at this stage in their lives will probably be included.

● A Life Mission Statement may go through many revisions throughout one's lifetime. Don't worry about that now. Just write it from the only perspective you have—what you know now.

● The most important part of this is not the result; it's the process. The thinking and soul-searching that is required for you to come up with your own statement is the real gold. But do write it down. It will force you to think harder and deepen your commitment to your real core values.

4. Ancient Wisdom

(The Scriptural Principle)

The book of Esther in the Old Testament tells about a man named Mordecai and his young cousin, Esther. By divine providence, Esther became queen, even though she was a Jew in a foreign country. An evil, self-serving man named Haman laid out a plot to kill all the Jewish people in the land. In a sense, he was the Adolf Hitler of his day.

After lamenting this crisis, Mordecai sent word to Esther and encouraged her to speak to the king, since she was in a better position than any other Jew to challenge this plot. She balked, fearing for her own life, since walking into the king's court on your own initiative was not exactly allowed. The law of the land forbade anyone to come unbidden—on pain of death. Esther wanted to withdraw and remain silent.

It was at this point that Mordecai spoke to her about her "life mission." He responded to her fears with a ringing challenge that built to a peak with this question: "Who knows but that you have come to royal position for such a time as this?" (Esther 4:14). Mordecai was attempting to awaken a sense of destiny inside her—letting her know that her whole life might be leading up to this "finest hour," this opportunity to fulfill her purpose in life.

Fortunately for all of us, Esther did act—and succeeded, fulfilling her God-given mission and saving the Hebrew race.

A verse to remember

"Who knows but that you have come to royal position for such a time as this?" (Esther 4:14).

5. The Closing

As you look over what your mentees write down regarding their missions, encourage them that this is a process. Many people, in fact, don't gain a full grasp of their calling until midlife.

Close with these directives:

● Suggest that they keep the statement in a place where they will see it, read it often, and review it.

● Tell them that you will be holding them accountable from time to time for their statement. Do this gently and graciously, however—don't let this become a club.

● Ask them to pray about their statement on a regular basis—that God would help them make it a reality in their lives. Tell them that you will also be praying for them.

The Ultimate Balancing Act

For Mentors Only

Have you ever seen someone whose life was noticeably out of balance? Chances are you've made that observation about someone who neglected family in favor of career, who ignored financial stability in favor of possessions they couldn't afford, who dodged physical fitness in favor of overeating or inactivity, who overlooked spiritual peace in favor of selfish pursuits.

People's lives can be out of balance in many ways. They can neglect one area, or they can overemphasize one area, which results in underemphasizing all the rest. Imbalance can vary by degrees as well, ranging from relatively normal to severely abnormal—the difference between a tire that is slightly soft and one that is totally flat.

This matter of balance is not easily recognized or diagnosed. It is somewhat subjective and legitimately varies from one person to another, one career to another, one culture to another, one stage of life to another. But it is a subject worth addressing because the resulting self-evaluation may enable us to make adjustments that pump air back into a deflating tire.

In this session we will emphasize two basic principles: balance and centeredness. We all have a hub, something around which our life revolves. It is the essential core of our being and holds everything else in place.

1. Introducing the Concept

Ask a series of questions

● Have you ever seen someone ride a unicycle? Have you ever watched someone who was just learning? What do you suppose is so hard about it? (Answer: There is only one point of contact with the ground—nothing else to stabilize the top-heavy rider and cycle.)

● Do you remember learning to ride a bicycle? Did you use training wheels at first? Why do you suppose they make training wheels for beginners?

● Have you ever ridden a tricycle—not one of the Big Wheels kind, but the old ones with the high seat? They were meant for small kids who couldn't handle two-wheelers yet, but they weren't very stable either. They tipped over easily and couldn't make fast turns without wiping out. They couldn't even make medium-speed turns. They had three points of contact with the ground, which was better than two, but still not very good.

● Do you remember ever riding a go-kart? Now that's a really stable vehicle. You can skid it and spin it, and it's just about impossible to turn it over. Part of the reason is a low center of gravity, but you can guess the other part...it has four wheels. That makes a huge difference in balance.

Just like a car with four tires, our lives have four basic dimensions. In order for us to be stable and balanced, we need to have all four of those dimensions working—all four tires on the ground. That doesn't happen automatically. We're not even born with all of them in working order.

Introduce the four dimensions

Important hint: Young people love to hear about their beginnings. Stories of their birth and the circumstances surrounding it do more than just satisfy curiosity. They help reinforce identity, belonging, being loved and wanted. So don't shortchange the next section by rushing through it too quickly.

We've provided the basic principles; take a few minutes to embellish them with some of the details (that you know or can guess) regarding your mentees' early life. Go ahead and picture the proud father in the waiting or delivery room; the tension that comes from excitement mixed with fear; the moment of birth—including complications, if any; the nurse cleaning, measuring, and weighing; friends and relatives coming to visit…Even if it is not usually your style to go into details and really tell a story, try it now. This has value far beyond the teaching of the balanced-life concept.

● The first dimension in life—your first tire—is the physical aspect. You were born and had immediate physical needs and awareness. Totally helpless to care for yourself in any way, you had only one point of contact—one tire. You were a physical life, period.

● The second dimension—your second tire—is the social aspect. Your social contact began with the doctor who delivered you, followed closely by a mother, who had already loved you for months. You were soon surrounded by relatives and friends who thought, or at least said, that you were the cutest baby they had ever seen. Hard to believe, isn't it?

● The third dimension—your third tire—is the mental aspect. Little by little you began to learn that certain behaviors brought certain results. If you felt a physical need such as hunger or even a social need such as companionship, you discovered that you could cry and someone would come running. If they didn't come immediately, you learned that crying louder would work. Your brain was beginning to develop patterns that form the basis of logical analysis. You were becoming a thinker—a real mental case.

● The fourth dimension—your fourth tire—is the spiritual aspect. Pretty early in life you began to know there was a difference between right and wrong. When you did something you thought was wrong, you felt a sense of guilt. There was probably some fear of punishment, too, but even without that, there was the ugly feeling of shame and guilt that comes when we violate our consciences. You had developed a moral quality—the beginning of a search for meaning, for good, for God.

So now you see the four dimensions of life: physical, social, mental, and spiritual. All of them are important and need to be developed in order for us to have a quality life as fully functioning human beings. Many animals have only the first two, and maybe a limited version of the third, but God has created humans with all four.

2. Truth Statement

Maintaining balance in life requires the pain of discipline. Losing balance in life results in the greater pain of rehabilitation.

3. The Lesson

◆ Option A: Take a field trip.

Go with your mentees to a tire dealer. Ask the service manager to explain and demonstrate balancing a tire. Notice what he or his mechanic has to do to balance it, the different size and heft of the weight-clips, the placement of the weight-clips, and so forth.

On the way home discuss balance in the light of what you learned.

◆ Option B: Take a "different" field trip.

Go to a bicycle shop, and ask the proprietor for a discarded front wheel that will fit one of your mentees' bikes. Explain what you want it for; make sure it was discarded because it was slightly bent or out of round. Ask your mentee for permission to mount it on his or her bike and suggest going for a bike ride together. Ask the teenager what it feels like to ride on the bad wheel, and let that be the springboard into the lesson.

◆ Option C: Continue the car-tire analogy.

Hint: You can help bring this to life by drawing some simple illustrations.

Have you ever seen a car by the side of the road with one tire completely off? There's no way you could drive it like that. Some people try to live that way, though. They completely ignore an important part of their lives and think they can get by just fine. Usually before too long, they come to a skidding halt.

But that's not the problem most people have. They don't try to drive with just three tires; they're more likely to drive with mismatched tires. You know those little doughnut tires used for spares these days? You can put one of those on and drive just fine. It feels a little funny at first, but you get used to it. The problem is that you can't drive on it very long—only long enough to get to a station where you can get a matching tire. If you drive on the doughnut too long, it will self-destruct or maybe even damage other parts of the car because of the mismatch.

Tires are meant to work as a team. Suppose you tried to put four different sizes of tires on your car—one original, one from a semi, one from a big tractor, and one from a 747. Of course that would be stupid, but that's what some people do with their lives.

More common is the person who tries to drive with one tire grossly over-inflated, one about right, one underinflated, and one flat. Not a very good ride. Because the tires are a team, the condition of one affects the others.

Now begin the application

It's the same way with our lives. When we think of the physical, social, mental, and spiritual parts, we realize pretty quickly that they are not independent of each other. They interrelate all the time.

For instance:
- How would you categorize school—what areas does it involve?
- How about church?
- Will the job you do in your studies affect any other part of your life?
- Is dating just social, or do other areas come into play?
- Is your thought life purely mental, or does it affect other areas?
- How about the way you manage money? What dimensions of your life are involved?
- What area of your life do you naturally give the most attention to?
- What area do you think you could get by without and suffer the least?
- How would you define the areas that have the greatest affect on your quality of life?

Imagine a successful drug dealer who has lots of money, but has to live every day violating his conscience and helping ruin the lives of people. Would you say his problem is a spiritual one? Sure it is—but that's not all. If you look closer, you'll find that his physical life is in constant danger. His mental life is filled with fears of being cheated or caught. His social life is filled with people who are friends as long as he has the goods, and the heat isn't on. Everything interrelates. A neglected spiritual life has an effect on everything else.
- So what does it mean to you to have a balanced life?
- Do you feel your life is well balanced?

4. Ancient Wisdom

(The Scriptural Principle)

"And Jesus grew in wisdom (mental) and stature (physical), and in favor with God (spiritual) and men (social)" (Luke 2:52).

One of the most powerful pieces of wisdom ever spoken came from the lips of Jesus. And, as usual, it seems backwards. After talking at great length about our social, mental, and physical needs, he comes up with this summary in Matthew 6:32-33...

Verses to remember

"Your heavenly Father already knows all your needs, and he will give you all you need from day to day if you live for him and make the Kingdom of God your primary concern" (Matthew 6:32-33, NLT).

5. The Closing

Each of us has only one center, one "first place" in our lives. This center is our highest value. If everything we have were stripped away one piece at a time, and we had the right to choose in which order the pieces were taken, the single thing we had left at the end would be our center.

Think of it as your hub, the thing around which your life revolves. What is it for you? Can you identify it? This is a terribly important question. If you're fuzzy on the answer, keep thinking.

Do you have something at the center that is not worthy of that honor? Do you have something there that can break, rust, rot, be taken, or die? Of all the things we treasure in life—our health, family, friends, wealth, power, fame—none of them comes with any guarantee. God says if we put him first—make him the center, the hub—he will see that we have everything else we need.

Draw a simple picture

Your life is like a wheel. Ideally you have God as the hub. The rim represents the rest of your spiritual life (your conscience, the fruit of the Spirit, etc.) The tire that surrounds the rim can be divided into the other three dimensions (physical, social, mental), showing that they all relate to each other as well as to the spiritual.

The last thing we need to complete the drawing is a set of spokes connecting the hub (at the center) with the rim. These spokes represent the way our spiritual life is nourished by God. We need regular times of Bible reading, prayer, giving, and fellowship at church in order to keep our spiritual life healthy and balanced.

Maybe today you want to make sure that God is at the hub of your life. If you sense that something else is in that spot, choose now to give it to God.

Maybe you have done that in the past, but you realize that your life is not in balance now—you've neglected the spokes that connect the hub with the rest of your life. Make the choice to begin a new pattern. It doesn't have to be a huge time commitment—but it needs to be enough that you know without a doubt he's at the hub and you are in balance.

What we've learned

The four dimensions of life are so interwoven that we cannot separate them. One thing affects the next. In the final analysis it is the spiritual part of our life that defines the essence of who we are. It is the part that determines our values and dictates our priorities. God, as our designer, is the only one who qualifies to be the hub, keeping the other dimensions in balance.

Practice What You Preach

Conviction

For Mentors Only

Every one of us is responsible to have values in our life and pass on those values to our sphere of influence. Specifically, our children and those we mentor should see us living what we believe.

In this lesson we will learn more about our inner values and how to pass them along. Some practical points:

- Our actions speak louder than our words.
- Christianity is more caught than taught.
- People do what people see.
- The people who live with me really know me. What do they think?

1. Introducing the Concept

◆ Option A: Tell this story.

Tell this personal story from Dan Seaborn, the author of this session:

A few months ago my wife and I found ourselves in the middle of a heated argument. Our oldest son was within earshot and heard most of our conversation.

At one point I was quite frustrated and stomped out of the living room into the kitchen. I stood there, leaning against the counter with my arms folded and a look of frustration across my face. My son walked into the room and looked at me with a questioning expression.

I looked sternly at him and said, "What?"

He hadn't asked a question, but I could tell he wanted to. With a sense of reservation he asked, "Dad, why is it you can act this way, but you won't let me?"

He caught me off guard. He was right. I expect him to live a certain way and value good behavior, but I wasn't living by the same standard. I apologized to him, and I apologized to his mom. They both forgave me.

◆ Option B: Share this notable quote.

David Robinson, center for the NBA's San Antonio Spurs, told USA Today: "Being a father and husband is it. Those are probably the two hardest things to do because those are every day. [On the court,] the cameras are on you only about 10 percent of the time, but at home they're on you all the time. You can't fool your wife and you can't fool your kids.

"Laying the foundation for that stuff is the thing I'm most proud of, because that's who I am and that's the legacy I'm going to leave. This basketball stuff is fun, and I'm going to accomplish more things, but I don't think people will remember me so much for this as they will for the way I live my life."

◆ Option C: Go outside.

Take your mentees to a historical site near your home—maybe a monument or a cemetery. In advance, think of the values of the person to whom this site is dedicated. If a monument, what did the person do that caused people to value him or her enough to erect the monument? If a tombstone, what were the values of the person?

When you leave the site, allow your mentees to take a stone or other item from the surrounding area as a reminder of your visit there. Talk about the values this person held that you want to practice in your life.

2. Truth Statement

What you say will fade away, but what you do will show right through.

3. The Lesson

Talk about the Robinson quote

After reading aloud what David Robinson said, ask these questions (perhaps as you shoot hoops together):

● What do you think life is like for David Robinson? (Help them see all angles of a sports hero's life.)

● Would you like to live that kind of life? Why or why not?

● We all look up to these kinds of heroes. Who do you think looks up to you?

Find a quiet place

Sit down with your mentees and ask these deeper questions. (It's important that nothing distract your time together. Make sure it's comfortable for talking—in other words, a safe place you both enjoy.)

● What values do you see in me that you like?

● What could I do to improve some of my values? (Give your mentees freedom to be honest. When you show a teachable spirit, you are doing some of the best mentoring possible!)

● What values do you want to build into your life?

● Who is somebody whose values you really admire? Why? (Let the conversation flow. Don't get stuck on the questions—just talk openly.)

Make a list of ways you have seen your mentees live their values. Together, think of new ways to be a living example of these values. For example:

Value	Real-life responses
Honesty	Don't lie to your parents.
	Be honest even if it hurts.
	Honor others who tell the truth.

Series 2

The making of a finished product

If you haven't already taken the field trip mentioned in the introductory section, take your mentees to a local manufacturing plant or other facility that starts with raw materials and creates a finished product. Go on a tour (having set this up in advance). Walk through the plant and watch the raw materials become a valuable item.

As you walk and talk together, you build relationship and also learn about the process of manufacturing this product. Talk about the reason for its value. Why is it made? Who benefits from having this product?

After your visit, move into talking about how people are made up of values. Over years of time we build a reputation. Sometimes the processes of life hurt, but they mold and build us into who we are. We are all in something like a manufacturing process. What we are living and what we value will be what we are remembered for.

Be honest about times you learned valuable lessons—even through pain. Compare life's lessons with what you saw happening to those raw materials. Share back and forth about these ideas.

If possible, keep a finished product as a reminder of your trip and your conversation. Refer to it when you see it on the shelf at home.

4. Ancient Wisdom

(The Scriptural Principle)

Those who do not practice what they preach are commonly referred to as hypocrites. Jesus accused the Pharisees of being hypocrites in Matthew 23. In verses 23 and 24, for example, he said, "Woe to you, teachers of the law and Pharisees, you hypocrites! You give a tenth of your spices—mint, dill and cummin. But you have neglected the more important matters of the law—justice, mercy and faithfulness. You should have practiced the latter, without neglecting the former. You blind guides! You strain out a gnat but swallow a camel."

In other words, they were not practicing the law that they were preaching. People are always judged by what they do, not the standards they verbalize. You've probably heard the phrase, "What you are speaks so loud I can't hear what you say."

A verse to remember
"Not everyone who says to me, 'Lord, Lord,' will enter the kingdom of heaven, but only he who does the will of my Father who is in heaven" (Matthew 7:21).

5. The Closing

Talk together about your experiences:
● How have you as a mentor grown in your understanding of your values?
● What did the mentees do today that they enjoyed the most?
● How will each of you be different in the way you live?

Pray for each other in this area of developing values. And the next time you see a mentee exhibit the values you are seeking to teach, take time to stop and celebrate.

Review, Reflect, and Respond

For Mentors Only

Not many people succeed in life while failing to keep day-by-day commitments. Remember this: A commitment is not really a commitment unless it is fulfilled. Commitment, by the very meaning of the word, is a binding promise.

This week's lesson again reviews what has been learned during the past six weeks. It reinforces doing what you talked about earlier.

1. The Truth Statements

During the past five weeks we have discussed the following concepts:

Inch by inch anything's a cinch, but what we often lack is help to stay on track.

The path of true greatness is hidden in the camouflage of humble service.

Mission is purpose coupled with passion, unlocking power to pursue God's plan.

Maintaining balance in life requires the pain of discipline. Losing balance in life results in the greater pain of rehabilitation.

What you say will fade away, but what you do will show right through.

Review each of these truth statements from the previous lessons with your mentees. Consider the following questions:

- What makes each of these statements important?
- How are these concepts beginning to impact your life?

2. Review

In the first lesson of this series ("You Want Me to Do What?"), you learned that big dreams have to be broken down into small steps, and then you need someone to hold you accountable for completing them. You carried a marble or pebble in your pocket for a week to remind you about this. How are you doing now, five weeks later? What progress are you making on the steps?

In the second lesson ("It's Your Serve"), you learned the importance of becoming a light in the world around you. You were told that you shine the brightest when you are serving others. Have you consciously made an effort to serve others and become a light in your world?

In the third lesson ("Developing a Life Mission Statement"), you began putting elements of your statement on paper. Have you worked on it lately?

Take time right now to review what you wrote a few weeks ago. Have any other thoughts about this occurred to you? Are there some changes you would like to make?

In the fourth lesson ("The Ultimate Balancing Act"), what did you decide about whether your life was in balance? Take a look at the drawing you made. Have you determined what your hub is? Review this together and then commit yourself to bringing your life into balance.

In last week's lesson ("Practice What You Preach"), you learned the importance of not only living what you believe, but also passing those values on to others. A columnist recently wrote about being asked, "Do you have any convictions that you would risk your life for?" He searched his heart for a few minutes and then said, "I would like to think I would, but that's easy to say sitting in a comfortable restaurant...In real life, who's to know what any of us would do if our beliefs were put to an ultimate test?" Discuss this together.

3. The Closing

After reviewing the previous lessons, reaffirm any commitments you and/or your mentees have made.

When you are finished, discuss continuing this mentoring relationship after a short time off. Decide on a specific date to begin again.

Winning the Battle, Losing the War

Courage

For Mentors Only

Our society does not exalt the fine art of conflict resolution, but each of us is aware that heated arguments...

- do not honor God.
- do not allow mutual respect to be shown.
- do not yield results that satisfy anyone.

Our culture is full of angry people shooting each other on freeways and in bedrooms, blasting each other on editorial pages and talk shows, and abandoning or divorcing each other with great animosity. Says one psychologist: "In the past 20 years, youths have moved from fists to automatic weapons to resolve conflicts. Their anger and flash point has lowered dramatically. They view teacher and peer rejection as undeserved, and they act."

Is it any wonder that many of today's teens hold little hope for the future? Many inner city kids do not expect to live into their twenties.

Your mentees know what conflict with teachers, siblings, parents, and peers is all about. But they will doubtless have little experience in resolving conflict creatively. Not only is this important for their day-to-day living right now, but any skills you can impart may carry into the rest of their lives, enriching relationships with a mate, employers, and colleagues.

Even in Christian work this will be an essential talent. One of the prime reasons missionaries leave the field is unresolved staff conflict. We are good at arguing; this lesson will give us better skill at reaching resolution.

1. Introducing the Concept

◆ Option A: Talk about family conflict.

Start the session by talking about a recent argument someone in your mentoring group has had with a family member. You might ask them when was the last time they argued with someone about music volume, who was going to use the car, or something else common in family life.

Ask these questions:

- What caused the conflict?
- How could the conflict have been avoided?
- What did you do to resolve the conflict? Or what could you have done?

◆ Option B: Go to court.

Sit in on a municipal court session with your mentees. If you spend some time in court, you'll run across plenty of examples of good and bad ways to handle conflict. Watch for opportunities to talk about the consequences of handling conflict in destructive ways.

◆ Option C: Watch a "gentleman's sport."

View part of a taped hockey game together, beginning at the point shortly before a major fight breaks out. Ask:
- Did you pick up on the cause of that fight? If so, what was it?
- What are the consequences of fighting in hockey?
- What would be the consequences if we all tried to settle our differences in real life the way they do in hockey?

2. Truth Statement

Conflict requires neither brains nor courage: Reconciliation requires both.

3. The Lesson

Conflict has many causes, some of which are listed below. Ask your mentees to look at the list for a minute and then pick the words or phrases that best describe the argument you talked about in "Introducing the Concept." Help them discover the conflict's roots.

Causes for conflict
Selfishness
Anger
Impatience
Frustration
Arrogance/Self-righteousness
Poor understanding of authority
Unwillingness to compromise
Illness/Tiredness/Depression
Immaturity
Lack of empathy
Differing ideas of how to do things

Discuss together how to deal with these causes when they occur.
- Is it normal to get into arguments with others? Why or why not?
- What sorts of things lead to arguments rather than discussions?
- At what point did you begin to feel anger? What was the cause of that anger?
- What could you have said to avoid further hostilities?
- At what moments might something different have been done or said to improve the outcome?
- What was the other person's perspective in this conflict?
- Is it possible to disagree and still get along?

Case studies

Now take some typical life situations where conflict occurs, and talk about what might be done either to avoid conflict or moderate its tone. You may use some of the following or come up with your own:
- Someone cuts you off on the freeway when you are late.

- A teacher whom you respect makes a negative comment about "religious" people being stupid.
- Your boss at the Hamburger Barn yells at you for leaving a mess on the counter.
- You run into your boyfriend/girlfriend sitting with your best friend on a bench outside of school—holding hands.

4. Ancient Wisdom

(The Scriptural Principle)

While Paul was in prison, he had a lengthy visit from a slave named Onesimus. (This story appears in the short New Testament book of Philemon.) Slavery was legal in those days. In fact, Onesimus's owner was Philemon, a Christian. Onesimus had run away and was subject to severe punishment if Philemon chose to exercise his rights.

This was a dangerous conflict, and Paul saw that as Christians, he and Philemon had a responsibility that went beyond the requirements of the law. Paul asked Philemon to forgive his former slave, and even to free him—to consider him as a brother in Christ rather than a servant. Paul offered to pay whatever costs might be involved.

Paul could have ordered Philemon to be kind, but instead he appealed to him on the basis of their shared faith and love for each other—a love that should extend to include Onesimus.

Verses to remember
"You have heard that it was said, 'Love your neighbor and hate your enemy.' But I tell you: Love your enemies and pray for those who persecute you" (Matthew 5:43-44).

5. The Closing

Conflict resolution for a Christian should always begin with prayer and submission to God. The prayer may be as brief and simple as a five-second thought, "God, give me wisdom and grace. Help me be like Jesus."

Then proceed to...

Confess your part in causing the conflict.

Ask God to help you see anything in your attitude that needs to change.

Ask yourself, "Does it really need to be my way?"

Commit yourself to resolving the problem and preserving the relationship.

Tim Elmore gives us the following eight steps for resolving conflict:

- Pray through your anger. Don't let emotion lead you. Wait until you're objective, but try to deal with issues before they become big ones.
- You initiate the contact. Don't wait for the other person to speak up first. Scripture beckons you to make things right, whether you're the offender or the offended.
- Begin with affirmation. Speak words of love and encouragement first. Then, receive fresh permission to challenge the person.
- Tell the person YOU have a problem or struggle. Don't say it's his

problem, but yours; own the fact that you have wrestled with this issue.

● As you bring up the issue, explain that you don't understand why this is. Aim to clarify. Always give the benefit of the doubt. Believe the best, and allow the other person to explain himself. Whenever you speak, be loving and clear.

● Establish forgiveness and repentance. Connect the issue you are correcting with who the other person is in Christ. Don't conclude the meeting until forgiveness is extended and issues resolved.

● Compromise on opinions, not on convictions or principles. Determine what you will die for. Be flexible with your opinions, but not with biblical principles.

● Pray and affirm your love at the end. Always close these times with prayer. Give hope and a future through your words.

(Adapted from "Mentoring: How to Invest Your Life in Others" by Tim Elmore. Copyright © 1995 Kingdom Building Ministries. Used by permission.)

Something Extra

Keep a journal of conflicts during the coming week—even small ones, and how each was dealt with. Bring the journal with you to next week's mentoring session.

I'm All Ears!

For Mentors Only

Successful people are good listeners. They understand the importance of taking time to carefully hear (and see) what other people are saying. They know that people talk in code, using their words, sounds, and body language to convey what they really mean. A good "code reader" is able to decipher these signs in conversations, understanding what the other person is trying to say. Active listening is one of the most important skills to acquire.

1. Introducing the Concept

Ask some questions

As you ask these questions, be a model of good listening skills. Be patient and wait for your mentees to answer, giving both time and space. Your entire body needs to be in a listening position, not just your ears. Keep your eyes focused, your heart open and tuned in to what they are and aren't saying. Watch their faces and bodies for information beyond the words you hear.

As they are talking, let them know you're listening by nodding your head, giving verbal affirmations: "Mmm-hmm," "Really?" "Wow!" "I didn't know that," and any other short statements that don't cast judgment, but show attention and interest.

- What do you think it means to listen actively to another person?
- What does a good listener do? How about a poor one?
- What does a good listener say? How about a poor one?

A mentor's first instinct is to run in and fix the other person and his problems. As good listeners, we need to simply listen to other people. When we jump in with our opinions, solutions, life stories, or judgments, we are telling other people that our feelings and opinions are more important than theirs. We are also causing them to rely on us for all the answers. This can result in being more dependent rather than less dependent.

You want your mentees to solve their own problems. They need to grow from the consequences of their own decisions. We should listen and give some wise counsel, but allow the main decisions to be theirs.

Describe some models

Tell about a person who was a great listener for you. Talk about how important this person was to you, sharing the specific details of what you liked. Talk about the places where you had your best discussions, the way the listener made you feel comfortable, and how this person encouraged you to open up. Let your mentees learn from your story the qualities of a good listener.

Then you may want to contrast with the story of another person who has been a poor listener for you. Be specific in the details here, too. Talk about what the person did that kept you from sharing your heart. What were the conversation blockers? As you critique, make sure you are critiquing the listener's skills, not the listener as a person. Some people are wonderful people but poor listeners.

2. Truth Statement

Talk to me and I may hear you. Listen to me and I will love you.

3. The Lesson

◆ Option A: Visit a retirement home.

Spend an afternoon together listening to elderly residents' stories. This is a great opportunity to put listening skills into practice. On the way there, talk about what it means to listen actively to another person. Reinforce these points:

- Maintain good eye contact.
- Care about what the other person is saying—it's important to him or her.
- Listen to what the person says, and seek to understand.
- Pay attention to the tone of voice and body language.
- Affirm that you hear what the person is saying by nodding, smiling, or giving a verbal response.
- If you are unsure, ask questions—make sure you understand.
- Rephrase what you understand.
- If you ask a question, give time to answer back.
- As the person speaks, keep quiet and listen, listen, listen.

◆ Option B: Do a role-play.

Show what it means to be a good listener and a poor listener. You be the listener and let a mentee do the talking.

First, be a poor listener. Look at your watch, glance around the room, act bored with what the person is saying, ask questions that show you aren't listening. Interrupt with unimportant comments. Tell about a time in your life that barely relates to what is being talked about. Tell the person her thinking is wrong and she shouldn't feel the way she does.

When you are done, ask how your conduct made everyone feel. What were some specific listening blockers you used? Did the person feel like stopping altogether?

Next, be a good listener. Look right at the mentee and maintain good eye contact. Be relaxed and comfortable. Ask questions to clarify a thought or a feeling to make sure you understand what is being communicated to you. Give constant feedback by nodding your head and verbalizing agreement so the person knows you are listening.

Sometimes you may want to rephrase something to make sure you understand. Accept whatever you hear as very important to the speaker. You don't have to agree with everything, but do keep listening.

The greatest way to influence mentees' listening skills is to model good listening skills for them. Listening begins when the listener sets the stage for conversation and makes the other person comfortable enough to share his or her heart. Pay attention to the environment. Sometimes an open conversation can occur in a fast-food restaurant, but other times it needs to be in a more private place. Be sensitive to the other person.

When your role-play is finished, talk about good listening and how it made them feel. What does a good listener do and say? Contrast the good listener with the poor listener. Even while debriefing the activity, make sure you are listening carefully and not running the conversation. Talk about how the good listener tries to decipher not only what is being said, but the meaning and feelings behind the words as well.

◆ Option C: Make a chart with two lists.

On one side write the characteristics of a good listener, on the other, the characteristics of a poor listener. Encourage your mentees to continue with the positive qualities, and ask how you can work together on the bad habits.

◆ Option D: Discuss these questions:

- What does a good listener do?
- What does a good listener say?
- Why do people want someone to listen to them?
- How do you feel when someone listens to you?
- How do you feel when someone doesn't listen to you?
- How can you be a better listener?

4. Ancient Wisdom

(The Scriptural Principle)

When Jesus was approached by the Pharisees about paying taxes to Caesar (see Matthew 22:15-22), it was not his first encounter with them. He had spent time with them and knew how they thought and acted. He knew the Pharisees were not interested in information on tax compliance, but rather wanted to trap, discredit, and accuse him.

Even though their words may have sounded innocent, Jesus was deciphering their intentions. After hearing them carefully, he answered them, "Give to Caesar what is Caesar's, and to God what is God's." Jesus listened, deciphered, and then responded.

This is a wonderful example of how we all need to conduct ourselves in conversation.

A verse to remember
"My dear brothers, take note of this: Everyone should be quick to listen, slow to speak and slow to become angry" (James 1:19).

5. The Closing

In this lesson you have learned by experience to be more of a listener. You know the importance of concentrating on what is being said. You have also learned that it is important to listen to what is being nonverbally communicated.

Now all you have to do is put this into practice!

A Master Plan for Your Life

Competency

For Mentors Only

As the old saying goes, "If you aim at nothing, you'll probably hit it." One of the most important things a person can do to shape the outcome of life is to develop a Master Plan.

Of course this plan will shift and adjust to developing circumstances. Nevertheless, it serves as a source of direction and stability, giving guidance to what might otherwise be unfocused drifting.

This week's mentoring time should help your mentees learn the importance of having a plan and give some guidelines for developing one.

1. Introducing the Concept

◆ Option A: Tell this story or one of your own.

When Charles Carson was seven years old, his father deserted his family. After that, Charles struggled to grow up, living at home, in foster homes, and on the streets. When he was in tenth grade, he dropped out of school and ran away.

Charles became a drug addict and a criminal. He stole to support his drug habit. He was arrested and sent to detention homes eighteen times for crimes including burglary, arson, and forgery, all drug-related.

Life on the streets was harsh. All around him, Charles saw dead ends, death, and despair. One day, as he walked the streets, he looked around and saw people "staggering down the street talking to the wind, not knowing who they were, their brains all whacked out on drugs. They'd be walking around for the rest of their lives. No job. Nothing."

That day Charles remembered God. He remembered the lessons his mother had taught him. And he decided to make something of his life. He began to dream of making a difference in the world.

His life began to change. His faith developed, and he began to think about pleasing God in his actions. He started to play basketball, lift weights, and play the guitar. Eventually, he stopped using drugs.

Charles realized his dream. He began to make a difference in the lives of other young people. At the Boys Club, he became a role model and counselor for kids. He went back and finished high school, then went on to college.

Charles went to work for the Tacoma Youth Initiative, recruiting troubled young people to do community service. He also began to speak out against drugs and violence on the radio, on TV, and through billboards. He's made something of his life, and he's making a difference in the world. He set a goal for himself, and he stayed on course.

(Source: *Kids With Courage* by Barbara A. Lewis.)

◆ Option B: Plan a trip.

Spread out a road map with your mentees. Starting with where you live, plan a major trip. First decide the places you would like to see or stay (for example, Washington D.C., the Rocky Mountains, the Florida Keys, Yellowstone, the Grand Canyon, New York City). Then determine the route.

The purpose of this exercise is to illustrate that in order to get to intended destinations, a strategy must be carefully planned.

◆ Option C: Use an object lesson.

Blindfold a mentee and twist him or her around a few times (not enough to get dizzy, just disoriented). Tell him or her to walk to a specific room in the house. For example, if you are in the kitchen, tell the mentee to walk to a certain bedroom by feeling the way.

Time how long this takes—probably minutes.

Then take the mentee back to the kitchen, and with the blindfold off, time him or her again on the same assignment. It will probably be finished in seconds.

Then sit down and discuss what you learned. For instance:

● It took longer with the blindfold on. (Anyone going blindly through life is going to take longer to get to the goal—if he or she gets there at all).

● The person was not as self-assured while blindfolded. (Anyone who goes blindly through life will always do it haltingly).

2. Truth Statement

Those who aim at nothing are sure to hit it.

3. The Lesson

Consider the following questions

As your mentees answer the questions below, it will be important for you to listen carefully. Do not discourage them even if their answers sound preposterous. Use additional probing questions as needed so that you really know what they are thinking.

● What kind of career would you like to have? (If you get an "I don't know," it might be because they don't think they could ever accomplish such a dream. Encourage them at this stage to dream with their hearts. There's plenty of time for reality later.)

● What are some of the things you'll have to do to prepare for this? (A typical answer will be "go to college." You'll need to press a little further—get them to think about the preparation, scholastic prerequisites, and exposure to their field of interest that would be helpful between now and then.)

● What do you see as the steps you'll need to take throughout your life to get where you want to go? (Remind them of the Charles Carson story). This is where you will begin helping them define the map of their lives. Allow several minutes for this dialogue.

Series 3

Mapping your life

Give each mentee a large piece of paper, and ask him or her to do the following:

● Draw an X (representing present position) in the lower left corner.

● In the upper right corner, draw a box and label it with your career goal, for example, "successful attorney," "astronaut," or "teacher."

● Now, between the X and the box, write the action steps that will need to be taken. These might begin with respecting parents (it doesn't hurt to try!), remaining honest, or completing homework, and progress to visiting the aerospace museum in Houston, majoring in electronics, and attending leadership seminars.

● Start at the X and draw a line to the first action step, then the second, and so on.

Be sure to point out that some of these things may change. The order may be altered. The mentees might change their mind about the ultimate goals. Regardless, here's what's important:

● Successful people visualize where they are going and how they can get there.

● Setbacks never stop the person of courage from adjusting and moving forward.

4. Ancient Wisdom

(The Scriptural Principle)

When mapping our lives, we must not forget who is in control. God honors the mapping of our lives when we align them with his will for us.

A man long ago named Solomon got to be king. (He didn't plan that part; he just happened to be born into the right palace!) However, once on the throne of his country, he made quite a name for himself with major construction projects. He spent seven years organizing and guiding the construction of an impressive temple for God. Then he spent the next thirteen years doing a knockout palace for himself. This man would have ranked right up there with today's property developers of world-class office towers, malls, and theme parks.

Along the way, as you probably know, he collected a book of wise sayings. We call it the book of Proverbs. Here are four important points about planning from Solomon's book:

1. It's a very good idea.

"The plans of the diligent lead to profit as surely as haste leads to poverty" (Proverbs 21:5).

"Do not those who plot evil go astray? But those who plan what is good find love and faithfulness" (14:22).

"The prudent see danger and take refuge, but the simple keep going and suffer for it" (27:12).

2. But don't try to do your planning alone.

"Plans fail for lack of counsel, but with many advisers they succeed" (15:22).

A Master Plan for Your Life

"Make plans by seeking advice; if you wage war, obtain guidance" (20:18).

3. Even with the best planning, leave room for God's "surprises."
"In his heart a man plans his course, but the Lord determines his steps" (16:9).
"Many are the plans in a man's heart, but it is the Lord's purpose that prevails" (19:21).

4. Whatever you do, don't be stupid enough to buck God's will.
"If you have played the fool and exalted yourself, or if you have planned evil, clap your hand over your mouth!" (30:32).
"There is no wisdom, no insight, no plan that can succeed against the Lord" (21:30).

A verse to remember
"We can make our plans, but the Lord determines our steps" (Proverbs 16:9, NLT).

5. The Closing

Spend a few minutes discussing these concepts:
- The wise person plans in spite of knowing that he or she can neither predict nor control all outcomes.
- A moving ship can be steered by a small rudder. A still ship cannot be steered at all.
- No plan is perfect, but even a mediocre plan is better than none. It at least considers some contingencies and provides some solutions.
- Many people say they would rather be lucky than good. Isn't it interesting how often luck follows planning and hard work?

Something Extra

In view of your life goals, both you and your mentees might sit down and map out your goals for the next six months to a year. When you meet next, ask them if they have taken the first step in their plans. Also allow them to ask you the same question.

No Pain, No Gain

For Mentors Only

The real test of our character is our willingness to take control of our lives. Discipline is not legalism or people-pleasing. It is embracing the freedom to do what is right.

Discipline is strength under control. You must enable your mentees to grasp the importance of bringing discipline to their attitudes and responsibilities.

1. Introducing the Concept

◆ Option A: Interview an athlete.

Have your mentees join you in interviewing a disciplined athlete, professional or amateur. Discuss with the athlete the importance of self-discipline in achieving success.

◆ Option B: Ask this basic question.

● What is the definition of discipline?

Listen attentively to the response. Focus on understanding how much they grasp the disciplined life.

◆ Option C: Relate a personal experience.

Tell about someone who really encouraged you with the importance of discipline or self-control. It may be a parent, sibling, coach, teacher, pastor, or youth pastor.

◆ Option D: Take a field trip to a health club or gym.

Participate in some weightlifting "reps" or systematic exercises. Afterward, discuss the parallel between physical discipline and character building. For example:
● Both can be repetitious and boring.
● We don't see results immediately.
● But without some pain, there's no gain.

2. Truth Statement

Until you learn to do what you ought to do instead of what you want to do, you will never want to do what you ought to do.

Truth

3. The Lesson

Select self-control areas

Have your mentees select several areas from their lives that need to be controlled. They may come up with
- the need to gain or lose weight,
- the need to exercise,
- the need to develop better study habits,
- the need to improve their relationship with parents or siblings, or
- the desire to develop a prayer or Bible reading habit.

The best way to identify these areas might be through using the following questions.
- What are some general areas that all of us need to bring under control? (Our bodies, our minds, our relationships, our faith)
- What areas do you see some of your friends struggling with right now?
- Why is self-control so important? (It affects our thinking, our actions, and our accomplishments.)
- What areas are you struggling with right now?
- Do you really want to become a disciplined person?
- How can you begin to develop discipline?

Choose some targets

Challenge your mentees to take some small steps toward control. Select one goal of discipline for each of the four areas you discussed back in Series 2, Week 4:
- Physical
- Social
- Mental
- Spiritual

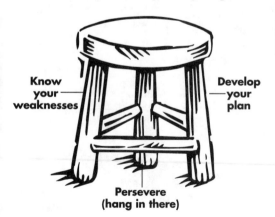

The three legs of discipline

Pull one leg out, and you've got a problem.

Know your weaknesses

Develop your plan

Persevere (hang in there)

Brainstorm some strategies to gain control. Examples: listening to helpful tapes or reading books, putting up signs or posters in your room, setting measurable goals with specific time periods, getting accountability for added strength.

Steps to self-control

1. **Know the areas of your weaknesses.** Pinpoint them. Begin with one or two, and prioritize them.

2. **Develop your plan.** How are you going to turn a weakness into a strength? Select a time frame. How much time a day will you give to this? How will you measure progress? When should you expect success?

3. **Persevere.** Hang in there. Do checkups on your progress. Discuss them with your mentor. Celebrate when you win over an area of your life to control.

4. Ancient Wisdom

(The Scriptural Principle)

One of the best examples of courage and the disciplined life is the true story of three teenagers in the Bible. They were forcibly taken from their country to a foreign culture, where they were placed in situations that could have compromised their character and destroyed the disciplined life they had known at home. Everything from the food they ate to their worship of God was threatened.

They had to choose between worshiping the true God or worshiping and serving the king. To worship and serve the king meant life; to stand firm in the discipline of their character meant death in a red-hot furnace.

The book of Daniel, chapters 1-3, tells how they stood firm on their character and self-control. As a result, they were tossed into the furnace—but, by God's intervention, escaped without harm. The end of this incredible story is that Shadrach, Meshach, and Abednego were given positions of honor, and their God became the God of the land.

A verse to remember

"Spend your time and energy in training yourself for spiritual fitness" (1 Timothy 4:7, NLT).

5. The Closing

You have attempted to make your mentees aware of how essential discipline is to building character. Encourage and affirm them in their self-worth. Help them know your desire to build character to a new level.

What we've learned

Everyone who has been truly successful in life has recognized the need for self-control. Discipline of every area of life is essential to success.

No Pain, No Gain

Don't Buy the Lie

For Mentors Only

Every day hundreds of thousands of teens put their lives at risk, not with drugs or gangs, but by becoming sexually involved. For some reason they have bought the lies that "Love = sex," that "Everyone is doing it," and that "If you don't hurt anyone, it's OK."

What young people need to understand is that being a man or woman has much more to do with their character than their sexuality.

This session will debunk three lies about sex and challenge your mentees to consider making a commitment to sexual purity and godly character that is both measurable and life-changing.

The information in this session may be difficult for you to communicate. Few subjects elicit as much interest as sex, while at the same time quieting a crowd. Just remember: Young people have very few places they can go for straightforward answers to their toughest questions. Pray and have others pray for you when you present this material.

Be aware that many teens have already experimented, may have been hurt or abused, or may be struggling with issues of sexual identity. Please be sensitive and Spirit-led.

1. Introducing the Concept

Ask some non-threatening questions

Don't overwhelm your mentees here at the beginning. The goal is just to get them thinking. Listen carefully to their answers, however; you may pick up clues to underlying assumptions and attitudes.

- Why do teens ask their friends for advice about sex?
- What are the limits of getting good sexual advice from peers?
- Where else do teens learn about sex?
- What percentage of teens on your campus do you think are "sexually active," as the saying goes?
- What do you think is the reason most teens get sexually involved with someone?
- Everybody's heard warnings about the two main consequences of teen sex: babies and sexually transmitted diseases (STDs). OK, what else? Are there other consequences besides those two? If so, what are they?
- Who do you think is more preoccupied with sex, guys or gals? Why?
- If a teenage guy on your campus declared his intention to remain a virgin, do you think there would be girls who would target him to get him to fail?
- What if it were reversed? Would guys target a girl who wanted to remain a virgin? Why is that?

● Have you known kids who were, or are now, sexually active? What is their story?

2. Truth Statement

Sex is fire: in the right place it is a beautiful and comforting flame; in the wrong, a destructive inferno.

3. The Lesson

Your world is full of lies. The media, music, and magazines all have one goal: to separate you from your money! And they use sex to do that. They make subtle "if-then" promises that aren't promises at all, but are really just outright lies. They convincingly imply that if you drink a certain beer or wear designer clothes, then you will be popular or successful.

The truth is, the consequences of casual sex are major. Sex outside of God's design is like a fire leaping out of a fireplace and into the living room. It is no longer safe and cozy but destructive and dangerous. I want to share with you three lies that you need to be aware of.

Lie number 1: Sex is bad.

Sometimes it seems that the most common message from adults is one of guilt and shame. Somehow it comes across that sex is bad or dirty. Nothing could be further from the truth.

If sex were bad, like hitting yourself with a hammer—then none of us would exist. Sex is pleasurable and powerful. God designed sex for us to be fruitful and to multiply. He designed it so we could enjoy physical intimacy. And he designed it for marriage so that we would understand the love and passion he has for his bride, the Church.

Sex isn't bad or dirty, but just like any other good gift God gives us, it can be abused.

Lie number 2: Sex = Love, and Love = Sex.

Here's a letter that a girl named Alysia sent to the Public Health Service's Office of Population Control. Listen to what she wrote:

Dear Public Health Service,

I've constantly been thinking about some advice I've received from some friends and a school counselor. I'm 15 and still a virgin. Sure, I've dated guys, and kissing guys isn't any big deal, but I haven't been into guys putting their hands all over my body or having a sexual relationship at this stage in my life.

Lately that has been the issue. Is there something wrong with my discomfort? I keep asking myself this question over and over again. All my friends talk about sex as if it has no emotional effect on them. Anyway, here is my situation:

I have been dating the captain of the football team for some time now. He has been coming on to me in the strangest places, like football games. He puts his hands up under my shirt and puts his hands on my breasts. After a couple of times of my telling him to stop, he gets mad.

90

It's like he is trying to show me off to his friends. After the games we usually go to a party in honor of the football team, and he always tries to get me aside into a bedroom, or if there aren't any rooms, we go to his car, where he tries to relieve my body of my clothes. I try telling him that I'm not ready, but it is hard. He is always telling me that if I love him I will understand what he needs and give him sex. When I tell him that I do love him and I do understand, but that I can't give him sex, he automatically returns to "You don't love me" or "You don't understand a male's needs." As soon as he figures out that that line doesn't work, he accuses me of seeing another guy.

My friends tell me to go ahead and have sex with him, because if I don't I'm going to lose him. Having sex is still against my will, because I am not positively sure I can take full responsibility for my actions. But I love him and I don't want to lose him.

I received this address through a school guidance counselor. I have talked to my counselor about other problems, but I couldn't get the nerve to talk about this. I would appreciate it if your service would send me some pamphlets on sexually transmitted diseases and the effectiveness of condoms and which brand of condoms might be more effective.

Sincerely, Alysia

Ask your mentees the following questions:
- If Alysia decides to have sex, will it be because she chooses to?
- What would you say to Alysia?

All too often teens come to believe that sex and love are the same. They are not. God intended sex to be a gift for you and your spouse in a marriage relationship. Even married people find that there are times when sex has to be put on hold for a while (like, when one person is traveling or one person is ill). To believe that sex is love and that it can be righteously enjoyed outside of marriage is to believe a lie. It is not just second-best, it is a sin, even if it feels like love.

Lie number 3: If no one gets hurt, it's OK.

The media seem to show extramarital sex as though it has no consequences. What a devastating lie! We've already mentioned babies and STDs, but there are many other negative results. How about financial distress, disappointed or angry parents, letdown friends, a ruined relationship with the person you had sex with, jail, guilt, and a broken relationship with God? How about having to explain to the person you are going to marry that you have a sexually transmitted disease and that someday he or she will have it too?

Just because the consequences are postponed doesn't mean they don't exist. Over 80 percent of the fifty-plus sexually transmitted diseases have no visible symptoms, and many can lead to sterility, cancer, and even death. Meanwhile, the emotional scars can be lifelong. Futures can be destroyed.

So how do you deal with the lies?

Set boundaries now

Here are some good ideas, some boundaries, that you need to set in your dating relationships. They will help you be true to your word and to God's Word.

1. Delay dating and going steady. Teens who wait until they are 16 or 17 to "go steady" have a much greater chance of remaining pure.

2. Don't drink and date. Alcohol puts you out of control and threatens you in many ways.

3. Group-date as often as you can. There is safety in numbers and in public settings.

4. Set a standard of which others are aware. Consider signing a pledge card like the one below, and let others (including those you date) know it is your intent to remain a virgin from this day on until marriage.

5. Nail this down in your mind: If anything gets unbuttoned, unzipped, or undone, you have gone too far. All clothing (both his and hers) must stay in its original location. Make this your last stand against a mistake. Go ahead and say it to those you date. Decide now, before you have to, that you will not let this kind of activity happen.

Worth Waiting For!

Believing that God's best is worth waiting for, I make a commitment to God, myself, my family, those I date, my future mate, and my future children to be sexually pure until the day I enter a covenant marriage relationship.

Signed _____ Date _____

---

4. Ancient Wisdom

(The Scriptural Principle)

The Bible speaks very openly about sexuality. It neither hides nor excuses the failures of some of its leading characters. It flatly condemns many practices that are widespread around the world.

At the same time, it elevates the importance of sexual intimacy between a married man and woman to a level the world doesn't imagine. God created sex to be a holistic event, one that combines the elements of real love (trust, commitment, emotional and spiritual union, care and willingness to sacrifice for the other) with the excitement he built into the biological experience.

Sexual activity outside of this provision may be temporarily exhilarating, but it always leads to regret, emptiness, feelings of guilt, emotional scars, and sometimes severe physical consequences. For a sobering look at the progression into sin's deception and darkness, read Romans 1:18-2:16.

A good follow-up passage is 1 Corinthians 6:9-20. Notice the power and uniqueness of verse 18, where Paul warns, "Flee from sexual immorality. All other sins a man commits are outside his body, but he who sins sexually sins against his own body." Many interpretations could be given to this text, but the serious tone of warning is clear. Should we be surprised at the consequences when we violate God's design?

Verses to remember
"Do you not know that your body is a temple of the Holy Spirit, who is in you, whom you have received from God? You are not your own; you were bought at a price. Therefore honor God with your body" (1 Corinthians 6:19-20).

5. The Closing

By choosing sexual abstinence until marriage, you are choosing God's best! Even if you have been hurt or forced or have made a bad choice in the past, you can live from today onward experiencing God's best: forgiven and free, healed and whole.

To walk the walk of sexual purity today, everyone needs help. Wise people recognize areas of danger or weakness and develop a plan that includes accountability. Here's a good example:

- You accept God's boundaries as your own.
- If you overstep his boundaries, you confess and repent of your sin. Then you start over, head high, forgiven.
- You let others into your life to help you and encourage you in a walk of honor.

In today's culture, with its deceitful philosophy and constant stream of illicit sexual messages, it is virtually impossible to live a life of sexual purity without becoming accountable to someone. Give yourself a chance. Make the right decisions ahead of time, and find someone who will help you. Positive benefits of two kinds will last the rest of your life:

1. Freedom from an array of negative consequences
2. Freedom to experience the ultimate depth of sexual experience once you're married

Review, Reflect, and Respond

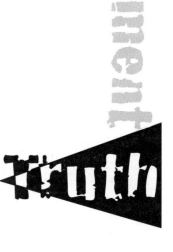

For Mentors Only

It's time to review what you have been learning together the last five weeks. In this lesson you will reinforce what you have been teaching and also assess how well your mentees grasp the concepts and put them into practice.

1. The Truth Statements

During the past five weeks we have learned some basic concepts about successful living:

Conflict requires neither brains nor courage: Reconciliation requires both.

Talk to me and I may hear you. Listen to me and I will love you.

Those who aim at nothing are sure to hit it.

Until you learn to do what you ought to do instead of what you want to do, you will never want to do what you ought to do.

Sex is fire: in the right place it is a beautiful and comforting flame; in the wrong, a destructive inferno.

Review each of these truth statements from the previous lessons with your mentees. Consider the following questions:

● What makes each of these statements important?

● How are these concepts beginning to impact your life?

2. Review

Lesson 1 ("Winning the Battle, Losing the War") was about conflict resolution. The writer told us that heated arguments...

...do not honor God,

...do not allow mutual respect to be shown, and

...do not yield results that satisfy anyone.

Meanwhile, conflicts are most easily resolved when...

...they are confronted early,

...respect is shown for others even when there are differences, and

...resolving the conflict is more important than your position.

It is important to commit yourself to resolving conflict early. That is far better than doing nothing and hoping it will go away. Pay now, or pay a higher price later.

Lesson 2 ("I'm All Ears!") should have helped you with what you learned in Lesson 1. It was about being a "people person" and enhancing your listening skills. Good listeners do not assume they know what the other person is going to say. They carefully listen—not only to what is being said, but also to what is communicated by body language.

Listening is the most important communication skill. Resolving conflict depends on listening and understanding what the other person is trying to say. How are you doing with the skill of listening?

In the third lesson of this series ("A Master Plan for Your Life"), we found out that it takes a lot of courage to sit down and think seriously about where you want your life to go. Many people live haphazardly, planning little more than to get up tomorrow morning and go once again to school or to work. And yet, something within us wants to plan the direction of our lives.

During that lesson, you laid out a tentative plan for your life. Are you feeling more sense of direction as a result?

Lesson 4 ("No Pain, No Gain") taught three important steps to self-control:

1. Know your weaknesses.
2. Develop your plan.
3. Persevere—hang in there.

People who have been successful in life recognize the need for self-control. The discipline of every area of their lives has been essential to their success.

Take a few minutes and study 1 Corinthians 9:26-27 together.

In the final lesson of this series ("Don't Buy the Lie"), we gave serious thought to sexual issues. We knocked down three common lies:

1. Sex is bad.
2. Sex = love, and love = sex.
3. If no one gets hurt, it's OK.

We emphasized the importance of setting solid boundaries before temptation arrives. I offered you the chance to make the "Worth Waiting For!" pledge. It's not easy in today's culture, but the payoff is far greater than any quick thrill you are likely to realize at this stage of your life.

3. The Closing

After reviewing the lessons in this series, talk to your mentees about the next series. Agree together to meet again on a weekly basis after a short break.

Finally, take time to thank God together for the things you've learned during this series.

Bouncing Back

Courage

For Mentors Only

What would you choose as the one single quality most responsible for reaching a goal or completing a difficult assignment?

Chances are you'll come up with one of the following synonyms: determination, perseverance, will, resolve, resilience, the ability to bounce back. Many of life's best examples come from people whose early lives gave them every reason to fail. They were abandoned, abused, handicapped, seriously ill, or suffered some other kind of trauma. Whatever the initial difficulty, they were determined to fight back. Gaining strength and confidence from early victories, they developed a pattern of not accepting any defeat as final. As Friedrich Wilhelm Nietzsche, the German philosopher, put it, "That which does not kill me makes me stronger."

This session conveys to your mentees a strong mental image of the resilient person. It encourages them to start making this a habit in their lives.

Many of the best movies and television dramas feature people who just keep on coming regardless. (You might cite a recent example here.) They are determined to not give up. Their path is hardly a constant string of victories. Often they are dealt such devastating blows it looks as though they will never recover. They have to retreat, scrap a plan and come up with a new one, find a new ally or weapon, start in a new direction—not just once or twice, but over and over again. Dealing with setbacks and beating insurmountable odds is what fascinates us.

Do you bounce?

Or splat?

Strong people don't have to be rude, insensitive, or showoffs; they just have a sense of being in control of their lives. They refuse to become helpless victims when life hands them a dirty deal. And dirty deals are inevitable. You and your mentees have already experienced some. They come in many forms. Here are just a few:

- serious illness
- the death of a family member or close friend
- rejection by a boyfriend or girlfriend
- the separation of parents
- being mugged, raped, or caught in the crossfire between rival gangs

There are also things we bring upon ourselves, personal failures such as:

- being fired from a job or cut from a team
- failing a class
- breaking the moral code by cheating, stealing, lying, or hurting a friend.

Bouncing back doesn't mean you never get hurt. It doesn't mean you are indestructible or have no feelings. It's not putting on an act or hiding true feelings of loss. Serious losses naturally result in hurt and grief. Healthy survivors are able to face their true feelings, recognize them for what they are, and then move on after a reasonable amount of time.

1. Introducing the Concept

◆ Option A: Rent a video.

Watch a "comeback" movie together and let it set the stage. Suggestions include *Rudy,* the old Spencer Tracy classic *The Man Edison, The Miracle Worker* (Helen Keller's story) or *The Dravecky Story of Love and Grace.*

◆ Option B: Meet with a winner.

Do you know someone who has overcome a huge handicap or turned a loss or failure into success? Could you arrange for your mentees to interview that person?

◆ Option C: Ask a series of discussion questions.

● Have you ever noticed the way people pull for an underdog? Or how they love it when a team snatches victory from the jaws of defeat? Why do you suppose people especially like a story or movie when someone is hurt or cheated and struggles back to win in spite of it?

● Who have you read about or seen in a movie who impressed you that way—someone who just wouldn't quit even when you thought their last chance was gone?

● What is it about some people that enables them to respond that way, while others wallow in self-pity over similar circumstances?

2. Truth Statement

Winners use setbacks as learning experiences. Losers use them as warnings not to try again.

3. The Lesson

◆ Option A: Tell a story from your own experience when you...

● were tempted to give up, but kept trying or made a change in approach and ended up either accomplishing your original goal or a revised version of it.

● did give up and later realized you could have succeeded. (Vulnerability such as this is one of the most valuable assets any mentor has.)

◆ Option B: Tell a story about someone you know personally or through reading.

◆ Option C: Tell this story.

Can you imagine being born with no right hand? Suppose you were also born with a right leg that ended above your knee. Those are pretty serious limitations. Forget about any athletics or anything physically demanding, right?

Try telling that to John Rinehart. At the age of fourteen he made a decision that would change the rest of his life. He decided he would no longer let others tell him what to think about himself—what he could or couldn't do because of his physical limitations. He learned to play the trumpet, and he learned to ride a bicycle. No, he didn't become a world-famous horn player, but he did become a pretty good bicycle racer. He currently holds six U.S. national racing titles and four World Bicycle Racing Championships!

Speaking to groups of young people about not accepting their limitations at face value, he says he is actually thankful for his condition, adding, "It would be much harder for me to get corporate sponsorship if I had both legs."

The Survivor's Edge

Leaders bounce back from failures and negative circumstances beyond their control. They have an attitude. They are survivors. They refuse to become helpless victims when life hands them a dirty deal. They are constantly developing their Survivor's Edge.

The Survivor's Edge is a frame of mind, a personal philosophy that does not shy away from taking risks. It does not judge an attempt that fails nearly as harshly as a failure to attempt. It is always learning. It is convinced that the response to circumstances is more important than the circumstances themselves.

Survivors	Victims
Are active learners	Are passive learners
Use setbacks as learning experiences	Use setbacks as warnings not to try again
Believe that their responses greatly affect the outcome of their lives	Believe they are at the mercy of the fickle hand of fate and cannot greatly affect the outcome of their lives
Want to make things work	Want to make excuses
Make new plans	Add new fears
Take action to make something good happen	Take cover to keep something bad from happening
Look inside for direction	Wait to be told before making any moves
Experience failure and come out better for it	Avoid failure at all costs, and it costs them everything

4. Ancient Wisdom

(The Scriptural Principle)

How can we see failures as learning experiences? How can we view problems as opportunities? We need confidence that the process of our lives, no matter how painful at times, will result in something good. Romans 8:28 says, "And we know that in all things God works for the good of those who love him, who have been called according to his purpose." Philippians 1:6 assures us that "[we can be] confident of this, that he who began a good work in you will carry it on to completion until the day of Christ Jesus."

A verse to remember
"And we know that in all things God works for the good of those who love him, who have been called according to his purpose" (Romans 8:28).

5. The Closing

Ask your mentees, "Can you tell me about anyone you know personally who has gone through something really tough and come out stronger because of it?"

What gives you the Survivor's Edge? The strong internal belief that:

- I am an actor on the stage of life, not just a prop waiting to be moved.
- I have value and worth (I am a child of God).
- Most mistakes will not destroy me.
- Wisdom is a valuable friend that often grows out of painful experiences.
- I am a survivor, not a victim.

Something Extra

During this next week take a minute or two several times each day to repeat those five lines to yourself. Allow your brain and your emotions to soak them up. Once internalized, you will begin to see both yourself and the world in a more positive light—one that helps you bounce back and even profit from things that might destroy others.

Turning on the Radar

Compassion

For Mentors Only

Have you ever known a leader who seemed interested in you only so long as you had something to contribute to his or her cause? Once the project was over, however, or you were no longer involved, that interest totally disappeared.

Many leaders are project-oriented and results-driven to the extent that people feel used and abused by them. They don't mean to be rude; it's just the natural expression of their choleric nature to "get things done—now."

Others have a blend of temperaments that helps them sense the hidden needs in people and to respond. They often seem to carry in their heads a finely tuned "Needs Radar." They can sense if a person needs comfort, motivation, encouragement, or friendship. While this may be an inborn intuition for some, it is definitely a skill that can and should be developed.

The focus of this mentoring time is on developing and using "Needs Radar." Your mentees may already have that gift without ever turning it on; it could be lying dormant or in an undeveloped state.

Here are some appropriate responses to needs in the basic areas of life:

Needs	Appropriate Responses
Psychological needs	Affirmation
Mental needs	Stimulation, knowledge
Social needs	Friendship, acceptance
Spiritual needs	Forgiveness, meaning

Gee, Dave—I'm sorry you're in so much pain...but I'm real busy right now. Did you hear I won my game today?

1. Introducing the Concept

◆ Option A: Ask an opening question.

Ask: "I've been thinking about how lots of people have needs that others never even notice. For instance, can you think of a time when you or a friend had a need, but no one seemed to catch on?"

Hint: Listen carefully to their answers. You may pick up something to use later.

"Suppose you see a new student get on the school bus for the first time. You watch him look around and then sit alone in the third row. Does anyone seem to care? How does this new student feel?"

◆ Option B: Tell your own story.

Perhaps you'd feel more comfortable starting this time by sharing from your own life. If so, tell about a time you had some deep needs, and nobody knew it. Relate how this caused unhappiness, dissatisfaction, or lowered productivity.

(Always try to fill personal stories with rich details, descriptions of people, and open revelations of feelings. Storytelling is like weaving a rich tapestry that turns out to be a mirror in which mentees can see their own lives.)

Or you might prefer telling the opposite kind of story: when a leader in your life with "Needs Radar" sensed your needs and began meeting them. How were you comforted, encouraged, or motivated? Your story can set the scene for teaching the principle that unmet needs produce frustration and often result in low productivity. Successful people learn the skill of switching on their "Needs Radar" to sense when a person has significant unmet needs and respond accordingly.

◆ Option C: Take a trip.

Do you know a person who is a good example of sensitivity? If so, take your mentees to see the person and ask how he or she does this.

2. Truth Statement

The ability to sense the hidden needs of others is a treasure costing only our self-centeredness.

3. The Lesson

Talk about some deeper questions, such as these:
● What kind of needs do people have that cause frustration and lack of productivity?
● What are the deepest needs people have—the needs they often never talk about?
● What needs are universal—you can assume everybody has them?
● Are there any needs that should simply be ignored—in other words, needs for which you just cannot take responsibility? If so, give some examples.

Tuning the radar

If sensing people's needs is like an inner radar, where we monitor their "coastline" and search for unmet needs, let's talk a bit about what the various "blips" on the screen might mean. Here are some "blips."
● A group of fifteen people are gathered in a family room chatting happily. One guy is sitting off to the side looking out the window. What might this person's needs be?
● A friend is sitting across from you at lunch, staring mostly at her food. She seldom looks into your eyes, and almost every comment is negative and accompanied by grumbling. What might her needs be?
● A young woman drops her books. As she is picking them up, she says, "I'm so stupid. I can't do anything right!" What might her needs be?

◆ Option: Draw a diagram

If you like to doodle, draw a diagram of an automobile with the gas cap showing. While you're sketching, explain that human beings have needs just as an automobile needs fuel (draw arrows to the fuel cap). When needs are not met, the person eventually "runs out of gas" and grinds to a halt; he's weak, he quits moving forward, and he's unproductive.

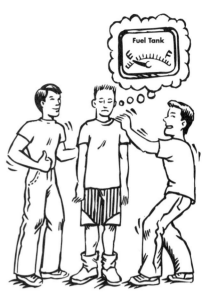

Leaders learn to sense when other people's "gas tanks" are low and fill them up—with encouragement, comfort, affirmation, acceptance, friendship, and significance.

4. Ancient Wisdom
(The Scriptural Principle)

The Bible tells in Acts 9 about a man named Barnabas, who had a great "Needs Radar."

Saul (later called Paul) had been persecuting Christians—arresting them and making their lives miserable, sometimes even killing them for what he thought was their heresy against the God of Abraham, Isaac, and Jacob. One day God chose to reveal himself to Saul in a shaft of light so intense it temporarily blinded him. He heard God's voice and realized that he had been violating God's plan to reconcile the world through Christ. He became a Christian believer and went to Jerusalem to see apostles such as Peter and John.

But they were afraid he was tricking them so he could kill them. They refused to see him.

Here's where Barnabas came in. His "Needs Radar" picked up on Paul's need to be accepted and believed. Barnabas was connected with the apostles, and he persuaded them to see Paul. As you probably know, this opened the door for Paul to become one of early Christianity's greatest leaders.

Barnabas was so good at perceptions like this that he later traveled for several years with Paul, starting Christian churches throughout Cyprus and Turkey. Barnabas' real name was Joseph. The apostles gave him the nickname Barnabas because of his "Needs Radar." The name means "encourager." He saw Paul's need and jumped in at a crucial time.

A verse to remember

"Do not let any unwholesome talk come out of your mouths, but only what is helpful for building others up according to their needs, that it may benefit those who listen" (Ephesians 4:29).

5. The Closing

If you are in a public place (a restaurant, a mall, a park), sit for several minutes and study others. Practice reading the "radar scope" of their faces, body language, or bearing. Try to guess their needs from just looking at how they sit, talk, and walk.

Affirm your mentees when they make a perceptive guess. Of course, there is no way to know for sure, but this kind of practice begins the life-changing habit of "looking at the scope" when you are with people.

If you are not in a public place and can't go to one, you can attempt the same thing by mentioning the names of people you all know and trying to identify their needs.

Something Extra

You might want to make an accountability covenant with your mentees for follow-through. Each of you could tell about someone in your life whose "tank is low" and go on to state what "fuel" you sense they need. Promise to supply that need before you meet again.

The next time you meet, start out by reporting how each of you did.

First Things First

For Mentors Only

Much of our personal effectiveness stems from the ability to get important things done. This presents two major problems. The obvious one is the need for discipline to follow an agenda that may include unpleasant but important items. The more fundamental problem is the need to define what is important in the first place. This may seem easy on the surface, but the common mistake of confusing the urgent with the important leaves many capable people neglecting their real priorities.

Two prior sessions, "Developing a Life Mission Statement" and "A Master Plan for Your Life," dealt with setting the agenda. Even though students are not yet at a stage of life where major decisions are theirs alone, it is clear that they get more out of education and life when they understand the priorities and have a hand in setting them.

If you have some weaknesses in your own practice of setting priorities and keeping first things first, it might be a good idea to mention it and make this a team project. Chances are good that the chink in your armor will come as no surprise! But your willingness to admit it and work toward change would be powerful.

Depending on how thoroughly you have already covered some of the material at the beginning of this session, you may choose to jump in at some point in the middle. We want to emphasize, however, that there are undergirding principles that must support any organizational system or time-management technique. Stated simply, here are the techniques:

● We generally accomplish what we choose to accomplish.

● Our choices are very important—they should align with our values, which should align with absolute principles.

● The responsibility for all our choices is, ultimately, our own.

1. Introducing the Concept

◆ Option A: Learn something new.

Work with your mentees to do some research on compasses. Take them to a library or a bookstore to read books on the subject. Find out how they work and how they apply to various activities such as hiking, sailing, and driving. Or simply interview someone who is familiar with compasses and how they work.

◆ Option B: Tell a story.

A bush pilot in Alaska was flying low over a wilderness area after taking off from a remote town. As he looked down, he noticed a bear with a garbage can stuck on its head. The bear appeared to be wandering aimlessly, unable to remove the can.

The pilot radioed back to the town with a message for the forest rangers, giving the bear's location. The rangers arrived soon, found the bear, and tranquilized him so they could cut the can off. He had apparently been rummaging in garbage cans for food and had wedged his head in so tightly that he couldn't get it back out.

That wasn't so amazing. The amazing part was that as they carefully examined his tracks, they discovered he had been helplessly walking in circles for over five hundred miles!

Unfortunately, people sometimes do the same thing, except for actually putting a garbage can on their heads. They waste time and energy going in circles because they have no plan.

◆ Option C: Ask these questions.

● If you were driving to visit friends in another state, would you just take off in whatever direction the car was pointed?

● Would you look for some other car that appealed to you and just follow it, hoping it would lead you where you wanted to go?

● If you had a plane and wanted to fly someplace, would you just go in whatever direction the wind was blowing so you could get there faster, or would you fly toward your destination regardless of the wind?

For the correct answers, turn to page...no, answers to questions like these are obvious. But sometimes we do similar things in our lives, and it's not so obvious until a long time later.

2. Truth Statement

Every hour spent in setting personal priorities saves ten in wasted effort and disappointment.

3. The Lesson

◆ Option A: Differentiate between the important and the urgent.

Can you think of an activity that, if you were to do it consistently, would have strong positive results in your life? Everyone stop...come up with at least one before going on, so this exercise will come to life for you.

(After you hear their responses) The bigger question is, If you can think of such an activity that would really improve the quality of your life, why are you not already consistently doing it?

In most cases the answer is, yes, it's vitally important—but it isn't urgent. It is something ongoing—there is no deadline associated with it. You have the feeling that you could do it any time, so you'll wait for a more convenient time, when nothing else is pressing.

Pretty early in life we develop the pattern of being governed by the urgent:
● deadlines
● cramming for a test
● demands and wishes of other people
● playing catch-up with things we've put off (last minute papers or homework)
● unwanted or unnecessary telephone calls

- junk mail
- too much television
- last-minute arrangements to fix something for which we've been postponing the routine maintenance (especially relationships)

Our lives get filled with activities that seem urgent, crowding out the most important ones:

- preparation
- spiritual input
- consistent study
- prevention
- sufficient rest
- physical exercise
- reasonable diet
- planning
- organizing
- prioritizing
- building relationships

Most important things, if neglected, will eventually become urgent crises with serious consequences. If, on the other hand, we learn to balance our lives with proper attention to the important, we can greatly reduce the urgent.

◆ Option B: Look at outcomes.

Often it is helpful to stand back and look at the big picture. What do you really want out of life? It takes a while to get through the clutter, but eventually you would probably identify three general areas of importance:

1. I want a good relationship with God (forgiven, accepted, in touch).

2. I want a good relationship with myself (clear conscience, organized, motivated, sense of direction/future).

3. I want a good relationship with others (family, friends, peers).

What will it take to accomplish these? If you come to the end of the week and you have spent no significant time in one or more of these areas, you are neglecting something important that is not urgent. You also will find, over time, that you are not getting the outcome you want. There are no magic shortcuts in matters that matter.

◆ Option C: Set goals.

As an adult, you may have a system in place that fits your style very well. If so, consider showing your mentees how you use it, and explore whether it would work well for them.

Most high achievers have learned the value of setting specific goals. Some do it formally, in a written and organized fashion; others do it more intuitively, on the fly. Committing goals to writing seems to bear a strong connection to getting them accomplished. Here's a very basic approach:

Look first at	Long-Term Goals (more than five years down the road)
Based on that, determine	Medium-Term Goals (six months to five years)

Based on that, determine   Short-Term Goals
(daily, weekly)

Keep in mind that goals are not mere wishes or dreams. They must be achievable and measurable—at least to the extent that you can tell if you have met them. For instance, to say "I want to have more friends" is a wish. To say "I want to make three new friends in the next six weeks" is a goal.

◆ Option D: Share these basic time-management tips.

● Use a weekly calendar or organizer with important (as well as urgent) blocks of time set in advance.

● Maintain a "To Do" list. Keep one copy at home and one in your organizer.

● Divide your study time into short blocks for maximum focus and retention. Approximately twenty minutes per subject seems to be ideal. Use a timer. Then stand up, stretch, go to a different subject, and return as necessary.

● Make it a habit to stay at least slightly ahead in your studies. Do tomorrow's reading today, for example. The advantages are remarkable. You will find that this habit...

1. Makes learning easier (what others are hearing for the first time, you are reviewing).

2. Reduces pressure.

3. Requires very little extra time (most of the extra time is at the very beginning).

4. Allows for emergencies without serious consequences (if something comes up at the last minute that prevents you from doing your daily study, you don't get seriously behind).

● Approach other preparation items in a similar way, doing what you can in advance so you allow yourself some time cushion. You never know when something unexpected will happen, or something will break, tear, or get lost, gobbling up time you had not anticipated.

● Keep a book, organizer, or note pad handy for times when you are at the mercy of someone else's schedule. Make use of what would otherwise be wasted time.

4. Ancient Wisdom

(The Scriptural Principle)

Paul compares setting priorities in our lives with preparing for a race. Listen to these words from 1 Corinthians 9:24-27 (NLT): "Remember that in a race everyone runs, but only one person gets the prize. You also must run in such a way that you will win. All athletes practice strict self-control. They do it to win a prize that will fade away, but we do it for an eternal prize. So I run straight to the goal with purpose in every step. I am not like a boxer who misses his punches. I discipline my body like an athlete, training it to do what it should. Otherwise, I fear that after preaching to others I myself might be disqualified."

Training, planning, and prioritizing always costs time and energy. But the price is dwarfed by the rewards of winning or achieving.

Verses to remember

" 'Love the Lord your God with all your heart and with all your soul and with all your mind.' This is the first and greatest commandment. And the second is like it: 'Love your neighbor as yourself'" (Matthew 22:37-39).

5. The Closing

Affirm the truth that achievement and freedom from frustration come by choosing the right priorities and following through with them.

Discuss this question: What steps do you want to take in setting your priorities?

What we have learned
- You generally accomplish what you choose to accomplish.
- That makes your choices very important.
- The choices are yours to make.
- There are no shortcuts in matters that matter.

Something Extra

Even if you have your act pretty well together on this whole topic, there's always room for updating and fine-tuning. Based on the response of your mentees, you might suggest putting some initial steps down on paper. Then compare notes.

Dealing With Attitudes

For Mentors Only

The main focus of this session is a simple truth: You're the only one who can choose your attitude.

Here are some practical points:

● You can't always control circumstances, but you can always control your attitude.

● Have an attitude of gratitude.

● Smile, and the world smiles with you.

Every day, when our feet first hit the floor, our attitude is beginning to be shaped. We get to decide: Will it be a good day or bad? Too often we let the events of the day determine the outcome. We have to decide in those first few moments to flip the switch in our minds to the positive mode. It is difficult, sure, but it's still our decision.

1. Introducing the Concept

◆ Option A: Tell this story.

[Dan Seaborn, author of this session, remembers:] When I was about seven years old, I was playing a game with several other boys from my church. At the end, I lost. The grand prize was given to the winner.

I began to pitch a fit, throwing myself on the floor, yelling and kicking. No one confronted my behavior. Instead, I was given a special prize to settle me down.

I will never forget that day. For years afterward, I kept having a bad attitude, thinking it would always get me what I wanted—until one day a peer stood up to me. I was terribly embarrassed. That was the day I decided winning and losing wasn't as important as my attitude.

◆ Option B: Draw an illustration.

Draw a large circle, and put half a dozen dots inside the circle as shown.

Ask your mentees what they see inside the circle. Most will say, "Dots." When they do, point out the fact that there is a lot of blank space within the circle, too! In fact, if we call the blank space positive attitudes and the dots negative attitudes…there's a lot more positive. But the negative seems to stand out.

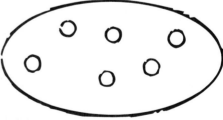

Talk about how we tend to notice the negatives in life and focus on them more than the positives. It's human nature to be critical. We must change this negative view within ourselves.

◆ Option C: Read Chuck Swindoll's quote.

(**Hint:** You might want to paraphrase this quote so it is more easily understood by your mentees. Some simplifying terms have been inserted for your usage.)

"The longer I live, the more I realize the impact of attitude on life. Attitude, to me, is more important than facts. It is more important than the past, than education, than things, than circumstances, than failures, than successes, than what other people think or say or do. It is more important than appearance, giftedness or skill. It will make or break a friendship...a church...a home. The remarkable thing is we have a choice every day regarding the attitude we will embrace [choose] for that day. We cannot change our past. We cannot change the fact that people will act in a certain way. We cannot change the inevitable [things that we have no control of]. The only thing we can do is play on the one string we have, and this is our attitude...I am convinced that life is 10 percent what happens to me and 90 percent how I react to it. And so it is with you...we are in charge of our ATTITUDES."

◆ Option D: Tell a personal story.

Recall a time you had a good attitude and what the result was. Then tell about another time you had a bad attitude and how things turned out. Share what you learned and how you would do things differently.

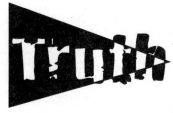

2. Truth Statement

Attitude is to success as wings are to an airplane.

3. The Lesson

◆ Option A: Learn from the past.

History tells us the average speed of the Mayflower during the voyage across the Atlantic Ocean was two miles per hour. There were probably times when every sailor on the ship wanted to give up and go back. Their attitudes must have "stunk." But that voyage is now remembered as one of the most glorious in the history of the world. It's a good thing someone had a "never-say-die" attitude.

Discuss the following:

● When life seems to crawl along at two miles per hour, do you develop a bad attitude?

● When you don't get what you want for dinner, do you have a bad attitude? Who do you take it out on?

Hold each other accountable this week in the area of attitudes. Agree on some "price" to pay (like a chore you could do for each other) if you have more than two bad attitudes during the week.

Consider this when you have a rotten attitude and want to give up:

● How do you cut down a tree? One chop at a time.
● How do you climb a ladder? One rung at a time.
● How do you eat an elephant? One bite at a time.
● How do you have a great attitude? One choice at a time.

◆ Option B: Leave your mark.

Each of us will leave a mark on the world. Our attitude toward life will decide what kind. Here is a description of the various types of "markers."

- **Erasable marker:** These individuals know when to put on a good front. They can show a good attitude when the right people are around, but when they leave, the attitude is erased, and the person goes back to being negative and critical.
- **Invisible marker:** You can't say these individuals have either a positive or negative attitude, because you can't tell what they think. They don't seem to care. Those who ignore or withdraw can cause as much pain as someone who is obviously negative.
- **Fine-point marker:** These people like things really neat and perfect. They are positive as long as everyone else is positive. But trouble breaks out if your mark crosses their mark. It complicates everything, and their attitude changes to the negative.
- **Highlighter marker:** These people have a good attitude only when they're getting all the spotlight. If they aren't the center of attention, it's pouting time.
- **Permanent marker:** What we all should be. These are people who make distinctive, lasting impressions with wonderful, upbeat attitudes.

Which of these marks are you making with your life right now? What type of "markers" do you hang out with? Are you influencing them, or are they influencing you?

◆ Option C: Go to a fast-food restaurant.

Go to a fast-food restaurant or another restaurant (your mentees' favorite) and observe people. Watch what happens if they have to wait too long for their order. Watch the waitresses, cooks, or cashiers. Watch how people react to others cutting in front of them. Who is serving whom? What kinds of attitudes do you see? What would you do in their situations? Who do you think would be the most fun to be around?

Help your mentees see that every person you observe is choosing his or her own attitudes. No one else can substitute.

4. Ancient Wisdom

(The Scriptural Principle)

Moses was the leader of Israel for many years. When they were first offered the opportunity to move into the promised land of Canaan, Moses sent twelve men to spy out the land and see if it would be good for them. They were to research the present inhabitants—their numbers, abilities, strength, characteristics—as well as the quality of the land itself.

Numbers 13–14 tells that when the twelve spies returned, they were carrying a cluster of grapes so big it took two men to carry it. Ten of the men agreed it was a wonderful land, but they were afraid the inhabitants were too big and powerful to overcome. The other two spies, Joshua and Caleb, had a different attitude. They were positive that the Israelites should immediately move to take the land.

Sadly, the Israelites decided not to take the risk. They ended up wandering in the wilderness because of their lack of faith until that whole generation died.

Faith combined with a positive attitude will help you conquer life's challenges.

A verse to remember

I can do everything through him who gives me strength (Philippians 4:13).

5. The Closing

Talk together about this lesson:

As a mentor...

● What have you learned about your own attitude?

● What can you do to continue to improve your attitude?

As a mentee...

● Finish this sentence: "I learned the most in this lesson when we..."

● How will you be different? How will you keep this change in your lifestyle?

Something Extra

Check in with each other next week and talk about your attitude during the past seven days.

Put a reminder in your room or on your mirror of the positive attitude you need.

True Blue

For Mentors Only

Leaders are often known for their strong and decisive manner. Sometimes relationship building is simply a way to gain allies in their push to be number one.

Contrary to appearances, people with conviction and compassion can finish first and be "the best" without falling into the routine of using others for self-gain. The value of good friendships—putting others before yourself—can become a regular part of life.

The focus of this mentoring time is protecting the integrity of friendships rather than tearing them apart by betraying confidences and exposing weaknesses.

1. Introducing the Concept

◆ Option A: Conduct person-on-the-street interviews.

Go to a school campus, a mall, a parking lot, or some other public place to conduct interviews. Have your mentees ask people what they think loyalty means, how they feel about loyalty, and how they've experienced (or not experienced) loyalty.

◆ Option B: Ask these questions:

● Have you ever made a big mistake, a real blunder, only to have someone you thought was a friend make a big deal about it to others? (You may wish to make this question more specific if you know about situations your mentees have faced.)
● How did you feel toward that "friend"?
● How about you yourself? Have you ever exploited someone else's misfortune or mistakes for the sake of your own attention or sensationalism?
● What effect did it have on your relationship with that person?

◆ Option C: Tell your own story.

Relate an example from your own life that illustrates the need for compassion in relationships. Sharing how you felt and the positive way such a situation might have been handled can be a powerful lesson.

2. Truth Statement

The first rule of loyalty is the Golden Rule.

True Blue

3. The Lesson

Talk about some deeper questions

● Why do people betray others by exposing their weaknesses or failures?

● How can a person change a bad habit such as gossiping, or always being anxious to see someone else make a mistake, or calling attention to the negative aspects of a peer or co-worker?

● How does a person decide when to remain quiet, when to encourage others, and when to expose the faults or weaknesses of others?

Explore these case studies

● A friend tells you she made an embarrassing mistake in last hour's class. She asks you not to tell anyone or discuss it if someone brings it up at lunch. What will you do when others try to draw you into a conversation about the person and the incident?

● Your best friend has just been jilted by another close friend, and the conversation turns to ways of getting even and seeking revenge. Will you participate, ignore the conversation, or seek to maintain a positive relationship with both friends?

● A girl you have become close friends with has no other friends. She has often been ridiculed for her dress and her "weird" personality. She confides in you that she is pregnant. Hurtful and mean rumors are now going around. Will you join others in their rumors or stand by her? Why or why not?

4. Ancient Wisdom

(The Scriptural Principle)

The Bible records a story about a young man named David who was given a number of opportunities to smear the name of King Saul. David had been gaining power and popularity. Saul was insanely jealous of David and was doing things that would have made it easy for David to discredit him.

In 1 Samuel chapters 24 and 26 we see how David responded to the opportunity to turn Saul's mistakes into personal advantage for himself. David refused to do such a thing to "my master, the Lord's anointed…" The Lord honored David many times for his integrity in not taking advantage of Saul.

In a parallel story, you can discover the positive attributes of friendship by studying the relationship between David and Saul's son Jonathan.

A verse to remember

"He who covers over an offense promotes love, but whoever repeats the matter separates close friends" (Proverbs 17:9).

5. The Closing

Each of you take this time to affirm the value of a particular relationship in your lives. How? By committing yourselves to do at least one confirming act of friendship toward this person before you meet again. Be prepared to share the results at your next session.

Something Extra

You may wish to keep a journal over the next week of times you had the opportunity to either tear down or build up someone, and how you acted and why. This can be the basis for further discussions on this topic of conviction and commitment to meaningful relationships.

Review, Reflect, and Respond

For Mentors Only

It's time again for review. During the last six weeks you've worked on some exciting material, no doubt cementing the bond between you and your mentees.

You have also come to the end of the first year's mentoring curriculum. We suggest that you review some of the highlights of your experiences during the past year. We also invite you to consider another series of lessons, after you have had a break for a few weeks.

1. The Truth Statements

During the past five weeks we have learned some basic concepts about several subjects, especially relationships:

Winners use setbacks as learning experiences. Losers use them as warnings not to try again.

The ability to sense the hidden needs of others is a treasure costing only our self-centeredness.

Every hour spent in setting personal priorities saves ten in wasted effort and disappointment.

Attitude is to success as wings are to an airplane.

The first rule of loyalty is the Golden Rule.

Review each of these truth statements from the previous lessons with your mentees. Consider the following questions:
● What makes each of these statements important?
● How are these concepts beginning to impact your life?

2. Review

In the first session of this series, "Bouncing Back," we discussed resilience. Leaders will often say that their setbacks have become their greatest learning experiences. Instead of staying down, they just keep getting up and going on.

Every survivor has learned these basic principles:
● I am an actor on the stage of life, not just a prop waiting to be moved.
● I have value and worth (I am a child of God).
● Most mistakes will not destroy me.
● Wisdom is a valuable friend that often grows out of painful experiences.
● I am a survivor, not a victim.

In the second session, "Turning on the Radar," we cultivated the ability to see hidden needs in others and respond to them. Once we discipline ourselves to look for the obvious needs, we soon find that even hidden needs become apparent.

At the end of the lesson, you were asked to think about finding someone who had a "low fuel tank."

- Did you find such a person?
- What hidden needs did you observe in this person?
- How did you respond?

In the third session, "First Things First," you learned some basic principles in priority setting.

- We usually accomplish what we choose to accomplish.
- Our choices should always align with our values.
- The responsibility for all our choices is, ultimately, our own.

When people set personal priorities, it moves their lives in the direction they want. Too many people allow immediate crises to rule their lives. By developing your priorities and staying on course, you can avoid "spinning your tires."

What have you done with the list of priorities you started at the end of this lesson? Have you made any adjustments since then to set priorities that align with your values? Have you seen any improvement in your time management? Can you think of any changes you might make now?

The fourth session, "Dealing With Attitudes," told us that outcomes are often determined by attitude. Most differences are resolved with a change of attitude. Relationships are destroyed by negative attitudes. Joyful attitudes are contagious and lift the spirits of those who are discouraged. We all determine our own attitudes and can often change situations by having the right attitude.

Did you put a reminder in your room or on your mirror of the positive attitude you need?

Finally, **last week** dealt with "True Blue"—protecting the integrity of friendships rather than tearing them apart by betraying confidences or exposing weaknesses and failings. Loyalty is not calling attention to someone else's mistakes, but rather framing what others do in the best possible light.

It was suggested that both you and your mentees keep, for a week, a journal of how you either tore people down or built them up. Did you keep such a journal? Discuss it together now.

3. The Closing

Celebrate together your completion of this year's work. Go out to eat, or do something special that your mentees would appreciate. Congratulate them for sticking with the process all the way to this point.

While you're celebrating, talk about the prospects for continuing next year. If there is interest, set a date to get together and make definite plans.

Emerging Young Leaders has several components available to enrich and enhance your mentoring experience with this curriculum:

Discussion-starters video: contains six brief segments to be watched during your meetings as discussion starters for six of the twenty-four lessons. Some are humorous, some are inspirational—all are thought-provoking.

Mentoring instructions on audiocassette: a combination of mentor training and inspirational material. It will strengthen your desire to mentor and your ability to do it with excellence. You'll want to review it periodically to deepen your knowledge and commitment.

"Life's Greatest Adventure" evangelism tool: the booklet around which the fifth session in the first series is built. The booklets make it easy for you and/or your protégés to share your faith in a logical and effective manner.

For any of these components, contact Emerging Young Leaders directly:

P.O. Box 3288 Englewood, CO 80155 Visit our web site: www.eyl.org
Telephone: (303) 771-3000 FAX: (303) 771-0933 e-mail: mailbox@eyl.org

Emerging Young Leaders also has additional mentoring guides available, some in print and some in process:

• *Successful Youth Mentoring,* volumes 2 and 3—the subsequent volumes of this material
• *Lead On,* volumes 1, 2, and 3—for international school and university students
• Guide for mentoring teen moms
• *Two by Two*—for married couples within the church

For further information, contact Emerging Young Leaders.

Emerging Young Leaders is establishing partnerships with churches in which EYL provides mentor trainers and training materials.

Mentor-training workshops for churches in your community are a high priority for EYL. The churches use EYL's mentoring curriculum materials and help underwrite costs for urban and/or overseas locations.

Another potential for partnership with churches is **The Mentoring Initiative,** EYL's global strategy for mobilizing mentors. Short-term mission teams can conduct mentor-training workshops around the world through the use of EYL's DVD training materials in multiple languages.

For further information, or for assistance in scheduling a training workshop, contact EYL directly.

About Emerging Young Leaders

Emerging Young Leaders (EYL) is a global, non-government, non-political, not-for-profit organization registered with the United States government and the State of Colorado. EYL maintains a 501 (C) (3) tax exempt status.

Emerging Young Leaders world offices are located in the Denver area of the State of Colorado, with P.O. Box 3288 Englewood, Colorado 80155 USA, as the corporate mailing address.

Emerging Young Leaders' board of trustees is comprised of representatives from each of the world's major geographic areas. EYL's area offices are in Africa, Asia-Pacific, Europe, and Latin America. The world office serves North America and the Caribbean.

Why Emerging Young Leaders?

"Leadership is always crucial to the church...but at the present moment, it seems to me leadership is especially urgent! Within the next decade, many of these "giants" [post World War II leaders] will need to pass on the mantle to others. They must harness the energies of younger men and women to disciple vast numbers of new converts, develop churches and evangelize huge numbers of unreached peoples."—Leighton Ford

Emerging Young Leaders (EYL) has taken a page from the life of Christ in establishing its leadership development methods: one individual building into the lives of others—one, two, or three at a time. EYL is committed to developing the world's emerging young leaders in home, academic, business, and church settings, using both mentoring and training experiences. They are recruiting spiritually mature mentors around the world to invest themselves in high school- and college-age protégés.

EYL's Mission Statement

To provide resources for mentoring and train the world's emerging young leaders for significant service and the development of others.

Global Outreach

International schools are one of the first global communities EYL is targeting. There are nearly 800 such secondary schools around the world. The students in these schools have a three-dimensional view of the world, usually speak more than one language, and are advanced academically. Upon graduation, they often return to the countries of their passports and attend the most prestigious universities.

Although these students have great leadership potential, very little effort has been given to evangelizing and discipling them. EYL believes these young people can be most effectively reached through mentoring relationships that have leadership development as their focus and attraction.

Group Publishing, Inc.
Attention: Product Development
P.O. Box 481
Loveland, CO 80539
Fax: (970) 669-1994

Evaluation for *SUCCESSFUL YOUTH MENTORING*

Please help Group Publishing, Inc., continue to provide innovative and useful resources for ministry. Please take a moment to fill out this evaluation and mail or fax it to us. Thanks!

● ● ●

1. As a whole, this book has been (circle one)

not very helpful   very helpful

1   2   3   4   5   6   7   8   9   10

2. The best things about this book:

3. Ways this book could be improved:

4. Things I will change because of this book:

5. Other books I'd like to see Group publish in the future:

6. Would you be interested in field-testing future Group products and giving us your feed-back? If so, please fill in the information below:

Name_____

Street Address_____

City _____ State _____ Zip_____

Phone Number _____ Date _____

Bible Study Series

Give Your Teenagers a Solid Faith Foundation That Lasts a Lifetime!

Here are the *essentials* of the Christian life—core values teenagers *must* believe to make good decisions now...and build an *unshakable* lifelong faith. Developed by youth workers like you...field-tested with *real* youth groups in *real* churches...here's the meat your kids *must* have to grow spiritually—presented in a fun, involving way!

Each 4-session **Core Belief Bible Study Series** book lets you easily...

● Lead deep, compelling, *relevant* discussions your kids won't want to miss...

● Involve teenagers in exploring life-changing truths...

● Help kids create healthy relationships with each other—and you!

Plus you'll make an *eternal difference* in the lives of your kids as you give them a solid faith foundation that stands firm on God's Word.

Here are the Core Belief Bible Study Series titles already available...

Senior High Studies

Why **Authority** Matters	0-7644-0892-5	Why **Prayer** Matters	0-7644-0893-3
Why **Being a Christian** Matters	0-7644-0883-6	Why **Relationships** Matter	0-7644-0896-8
Why **Creation** Matters	0-7644-0880-1	Why **Serving Others** Matters	0-7644-0895-X
Why **Forgiveness** Matters	0-7644-0887-9	Why **Spiritual Growth** Matters	0-7644-0884-4
Why **God** Matters	0-7644-0874-7	Why **Suffering** Matters	0-7644-0879-8
Why **God's Justice** Matters	0-7644-0886-0	Why **the Bible** Matters	0-7644-0882-8
Why **Jesus Christ** Matters	0-7644-0875-5	Why **the Church** Matters	0-7644-0890-9
Why **Love** Matters	0-7644-0889-5	Why **the Holy Spirit** Matters	0-7644-0876-3
Why **Our Families** Matter	0-7644-0894-1	Why **the Last Days** Matter	0-7644-0888-7
Why **Personal Character** Matters	0-7644-0885-2	Why **the Spiritual Realm** Matters	0-7644-0881-X
		Why **Worship** Matters	0-7644-0891-7

Junior High/Middle School Studies

The Truth About **Authority**	0-7644-0868-2	The Truth About **Serving Others**	0-7644-0871-2
The Truth About **Being a Christian**	0-7644-0859-3	The Truth About **Sin and Forgiveness**	0-7644-0863-1
The Truth About **Creation**	0-7644-0856-9		
The Truth About **Developing Character**	0-7644-0861-5	The Truth About **Spiritual Growth**	0-7644-0860-7
		The Truth About **Suffering**	0-7644-0855-0
The Truth About **God**	0-7644-0850-X	The Truth About **the Bible**	0-7644-0858-5
The Truth About **God's Justice**	0-7644-0862-3	The Truth About **the Church**	0-7644-0899-2
The Truth About **Jesus Christ**	0-7644-0851-8	The Truth About **the Holy Spirit**	0-7644-0852-6
The Truth About **Love**	0-7644-0865-8	The Truth About **the Last Days**	0-7644-0864-X
The Truth About **Our Families**	0-7644-0870-4	The Truth About **the Spiritual Realm**	0-7644-0857-7
The Truth About **Prayer**	0-7644-0869-0		
The Truth About **Relationships**	0-7644-0872-0	The Truth About **Worship**	0-7644-0867-4

Exciting Resources for Your Youth Ministry

All-Star Games From All-Star Youth Leaders

The ultimate game book—from the biggest names in youth ministry! All-time no-fail favorites from Wayne Rice, Les Christie, Rich Mullins, Tiger McLuen, Darrell Pearson, Dave Stone, Bart Campolo, Steve Fitzhugh, and 21 others! You get all the games you'll need for any situation. Plus, you get practical advice about how to design your own games and tricks for turning a *good* game into a *great* game!

ISBN 0-7644-2020-8

Last Impressions: Unforgettable Closings for Youth Meetings

Make the closing moments of your youth programs powerful and memorable with this collection of Group's best-ever low-prep (or no-prep!) youth meeting closings. You get over 170 favorite closings, each tied to a thought-provoking Bible passage. Great for anyone who works with teenagers!

ISBN 1-55945-629-9

The Youth Worker's Encyclopedia of Bible-Teaching Ideas

Here are the most comprehensive idea-books available for youth workers. With more than 365 creative ideas in each of these 400-page encyclopedias, there's at least one idea for every book of the Bible. You'll find ideas for retreats and overnighters...learning games...adventures...special projects...affirmations... parties...prayers...music...devotions...skits...and more!

Old Testament   ISBN 1-55945-184-X
New Testament   ISBN 1-55945-183-1

PointMaker™ Devotions for Youth Ministry

These 45 PointMakers™ help your teenagers discover, understand, and apply biblical principles. Use PointMakers as brief meetings on specific topics or slide them into any youth curriculum to make a lasting impression. Includes handy Scripture and topical indexes that make it quick and easy to select the perfect PointMaker for any lesson you want to teach!

ISBN 0-7644-2003-8

Order today from your local Christian bookstore, or write: Group Publishing, P.O. Box 485, Loveland, CO 80539.

More Resources for Your Youth Ministry

Group's Best Discussion Launchers for Youth Ministry

Here's the definitive collection of Group's best-ever discussion launchers! You'll get hundreds of thought-provoking questions kids can't resist discussing…compelling quotes that demand a response…and quick activities that pull kids into an experience they can't wait to talk about. Add zing to your youth meetings… revive meetings that are drifting off-track…and comfortably approach sensitive topics like AIDS, war, cults, gangs, suicide, dating, parents, self-image, and more!

ISBN 0-7644-2023-2

You-Choose-the-Ending Skits for Youth Ministry

Stephen Parolini

Try these 19 hot-topic skits guaranteed to keep your kids on the edge of their seats—because each skit has 3 possible endings! You can choose the ending…flip a coin…or let your teenagers vote. No matter which ending you pick, you'll get a great discussion going about a topic kids care about! Included: no-fail discussion questions!

ISBN 1-55945-627-2

No Supplies Required Crowdbreakers & Games

Dan McGill

This is the perfect book for youth workers on a tight budget. The only supplies you'll need for these quick activities are kids! All 95 ideas are fun, easy-to-do, creative, and tested for guaranteed success!

ISBN 1-55945-700-7

Youth Worker's Idea Depot™

Practical, proven ideas gathered from front-line professionals make this CD-ROM a gold mine of ministry solutions! You can search these ideas instantly—by Scripture…topic…key words…or by personal notes you've entered into your database. You'll get a complete library of ideas—plus a trial subscription to Group Magazine, where you'll discover dozens of new ideas in every issue! For Windows 3.1 or Windows 95.

ISBN 0-7644-2034-8